LIVING IN T[illegible]
FUTURE

Alan Radnor

ITV BOOKS
MACDONALD

Jointly published by

Independent Television Books Ltd
247 Tottenham Court Road
London W1P 0AU

and

Macdonald Phoebus Ltd
Holywell House, Worship Street
London EC2A 2EN

First published 1981

Printed and bound by Henri Proost, Turnhout, Belgium
Photoset by Yale Press, London

Distributed by Macdonald: ISBN 0 356 07542 7

(ITV Books: ISBN 0 900727 82 9)

Contents

ITV Books/Macdonald
In association with Thames Television

Who Wants Chips?

Nowadays we hear a lot about computers. But what are they and where are they? You may be surprised to learn that they are all around you. Computers can now be found in watches, in calculators, in electronic games like Space Invaders and television tennis. They can also be found in some washing machines and sewing machines, in toys and even in the latest cars. You have a computer of your own. It is working now, as you read these words. Where is it? It is inside your head because it is your brain that is your computer.

In fact, the brain is probably the best kind of computer in the world. We still do not fully understand how it works. But we do know that if our brains are damaged, we find it difficult to think properly, work problems out and remember. We talk about 'brainy' people inventing things. What they are doing is looking at a problem, thinking about it and finding an answer.

This is really what a computer does. But there is one big difference. We give it the problem, having already taught it how to work out an answer. A computer cannot be any more 'brainy' than we want it to be. It only does what it is told, time after time after time. Of course, if you have ever used a calculator you will know it can do difficult mathematical problems very quickly. It can add, multiply and divide the longest numbers and give you the right answer in a few seconds. But being faster does not mean being more clever. This is a very important point to understand and a look at some of the early computers should make it clear.

Most people think computers are new, part of the Space Age, and have not been around for very long. It is certainly true that without the help of computers, Man would have found it difficult to land on the Moon. But computers, which help us with numbers, are as old as Man himself. When Man first began to count, thousands and thousands of years ago, he found he could only add up to 10 using his fingers or 20 if he counted on his toes. For bigger numbers, he had to use something else. An easy way was

By kind permission of the Science Museum

The Pascaline

Room housing a valve computer

Piles of rocks, perhaps the world's first computers. ▲

Blaise Pascal's calculating machine, the Pascaline, is as primitive to the valve computer as the pile of rocks is to the Pascaline (top right).

The valve computer here was contained in a whole room at Manchester University in 1948. ▶

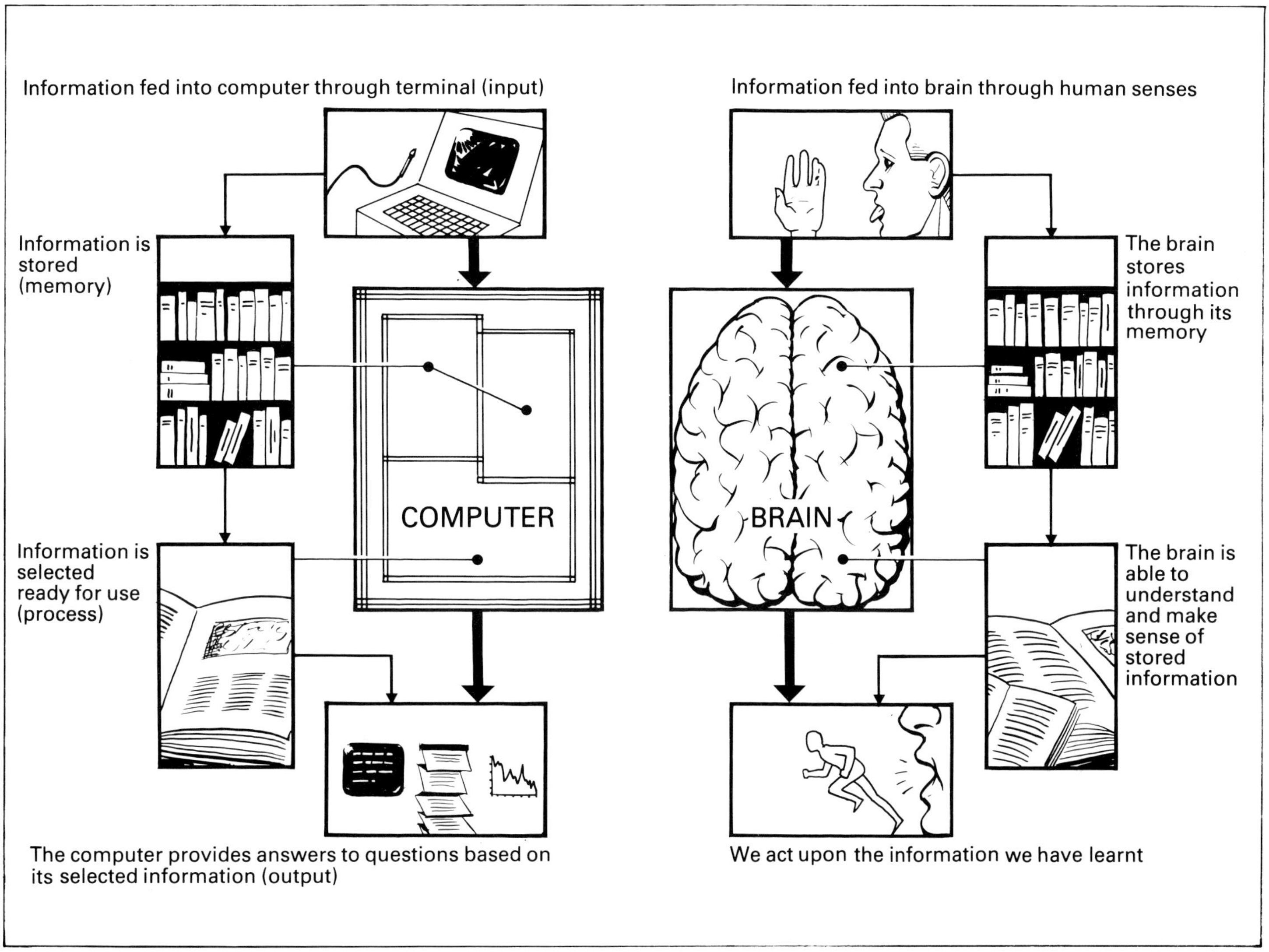

Information fed into computer through terminal (input)

Information is stored (memory)

Information is selected ready for use (process)

COMPUTER

The computer provides answers to questions based on its selected information (output)

Information fed into brain through human senses

The brain stores information through its memory

The brain is able to understand and make sense of stored information

BRAIN

We act upon the information we have learnt

to pick up a small rock for every 10 counted and build a small pile. If he was counting sheep, apples or people or anything else, all he had to do at the end was add up all the rocks in the pile to get the answer. So, it can be said that piles of rocks were probably the first computers in the world.

There were other ways that helped men in days of old when it came to remembering and working with numbers. An abacus is another simple kind of computer. It uses different coloured beads for different numbers, for example red for five, blue for ten, and so on. An abacus is a very useful adding machine and can be very quick in the hands of someone who knows how to use it. The abacus was used for hundreds of years and in some parts of the world it is still used. But as the world became more crowded, better ways of counting and working with numbers had to be found. Something new was needed not just to count people, although that was important, but also to keep records of

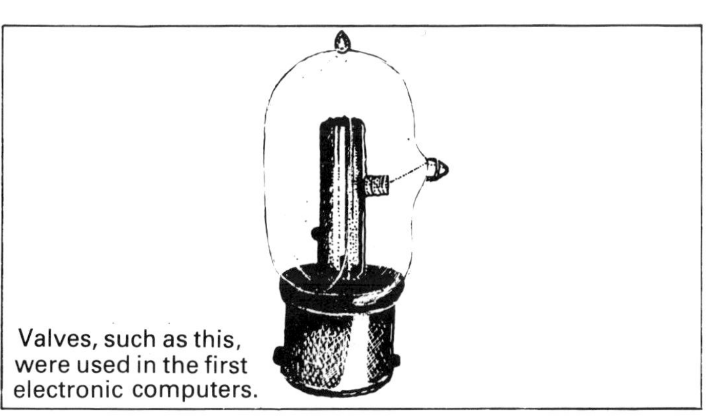

Valves, such as this, were used in the first electronic computers.

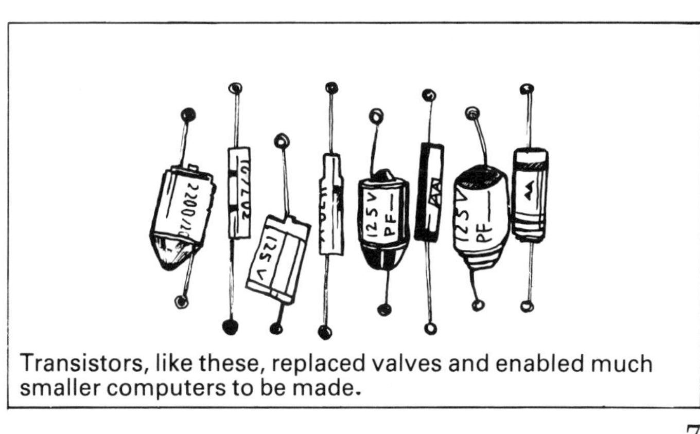

Transistors, like these, replaced valves and enabled much smaller computers to be made.

everything people needed, such as clothes, cattle, tools and houses.

New machines were invented which could add and also divide, subtract and multiply. In other words they could deal with arithmetic problems. It was a French teenager, Blaise Pascal, who invented the world's first calculating machine. As a young boy, Pascal used to watch his father, who collected taxes, work late into the night, trying to sort out all the difficult sums he had to do. Blaise Pascal felt there had to be a better way than the tiring, boring and slow way his father worked. In 1642, when he was 19 years old, he invented a machine that could add and subtract. This machine, called the Pascaline, could give correct answers in what was then thought to be super-human time.

After Pascal's machine, other people invented better calculating machines. The trouble with all these machines was that they had lots of moving parts and were always breaking down. They were **mechanical** and it was not until electricity was discovered about 100 years ago that this type of machine became faster and therefore better.

But it was only about 40 years ago, when your parents were children, that the first computer without moving parts was built. This was a completely **electronic** machine, called ENIAC for short. Instead of lots of wheels, rods, gears and cogs, there were thousands of **valves.** But, although it was then the fastest calculating machine in the world, it could only deal with one type of problem at a time. If you wanted ENIAC to work out a different kind of problem bits of it had to be taken apart and put together in a different way. It wasn't just a case of pressing a button or a switch, as we do now!

Although the valve computer was fast, it filled a large room, used a lot of electricity and got very hot, which meant the valves often burst. What was needed was something smaller than a valve, which would not use so much power, would stay cool and hopefully not break down. The answer came with the invention of the **transistor** just over 30 years ago. From that moment on, things were never the same.

Why did transistors make so much difference? For a start they were smaller than valves – 100 times smaller, in fact. Yet they could

This smaller computer can handle as much information as a much larger computer that 20 years ago filled a whole room. This sort of computer can already be bought in any good electrical equipment suppliers.

The hand-held computer contains memory chips and micro-processor chips. Combined they are able to store and deal with huge amounts of information.

ONE WAY OF MAKING A MICRO-CHIP

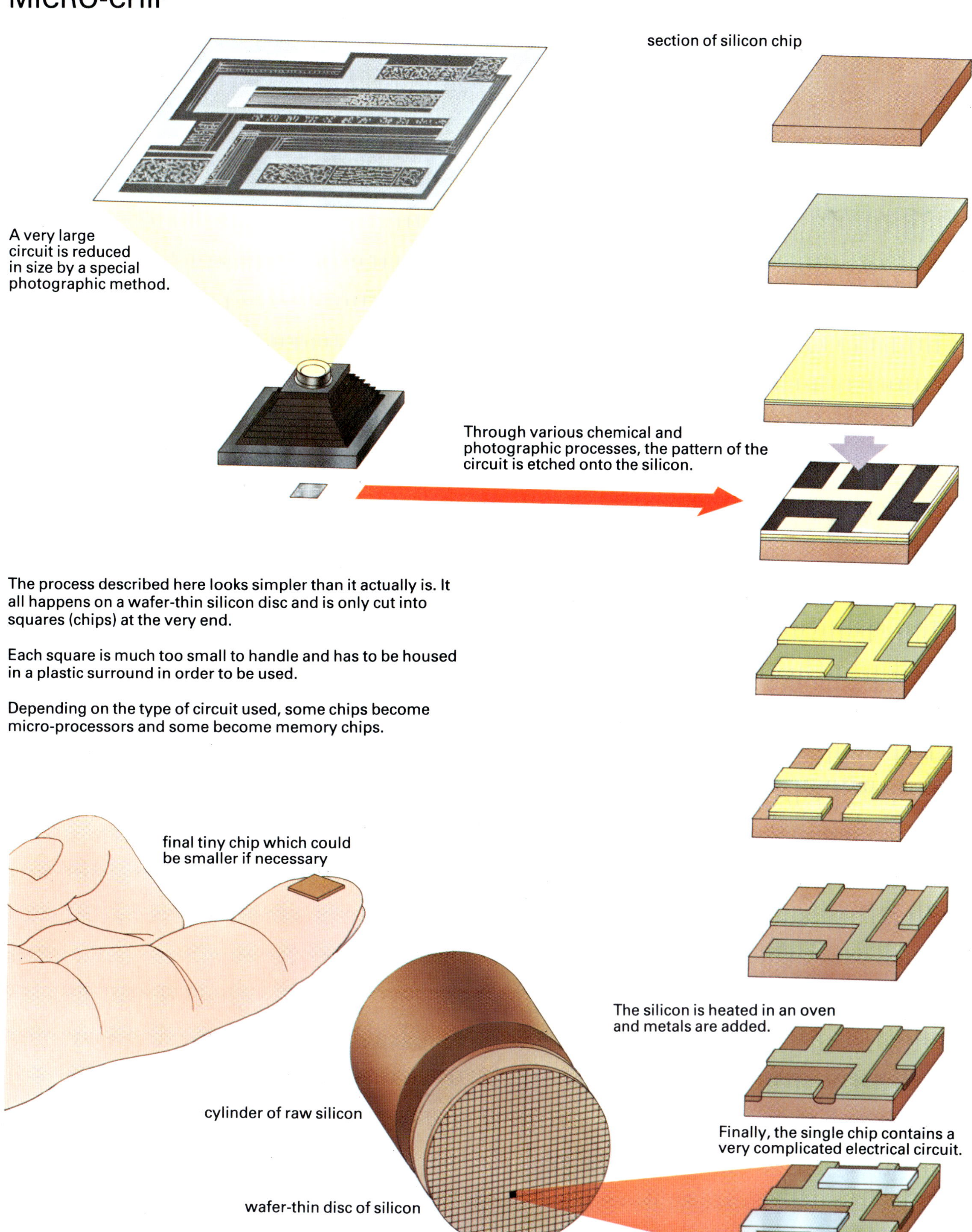

The process described here looks simpler than it actually is. It all happens on a wafer-thin silicon disc and is only cut into squares (chips) at the very end.

Each square is much too small to handle and has to be housed in a plastic surround in order to be used.

Depending on the type of circuit used, some chips become micro-processors and some become memory chips.

do the same work. So a huge valve computer could be 'shrunk' onto a small plastic board. Transistors were also much faster and did not break down so often. Their so-called **memories** were bigger and better, which meant information could be stored easily and found quickly. Until transistors were invented, computers were really not much more than calculators, working with numbers. Their memories could not store very much. But the new transistor computers could store many different kinds of facts. So in one jump we went from having enormous computers with tiny memories to tiny computers with enormous memories. Of course, with a better memory, a computer could do more than simple arithmetic.

In other words, computers stopped being number machines and became information machines. This was important and could not have happened without transistors. The world was changing fast. There were many more people and new discoveries were being made almost every day. Transistors made the world change even faster.

After transistors, computers went through a few more changes. New ways of building them were found, which meant they became even smaller. Instead of joining up different transistors on a board with wire, the joins were put into the board in the first place and then the transistors were simply 'slotted in'. These boards are called **printed circuit** boards. Then someone had the idea of making the boards even smaller and putting them on pieces of silicon. Silicon is one of the most common materials on Earth – it's only another name for sand. The centre of a modern transistor is a piece of silicon. One method of making these printed circuits very small is to use special photography. (Scientists are also developing another method with x-rays.)

Of course, you can't just take a handful of sand from the seaside and make a computer! The silicon has to be made pure and then moulded into little logs. Thin wafers are sliced from the log. Different patterns are then put on to the silicon wafer. In fact there are hundreds of tiny square patterns on one wafer. Each square is the same as a circuit board, only many times smaller. The squares are then cut out from the wafer and are now called chips. It is hard to believe that each one of these squares

MAKE YOUR OWN ABACUS

An abacus is a simple counting instrument. The black buttons or beads on the top line each represent one 'unit'. There are 10 buttons, so together they add up to 10. The second line has grey buttons and each of these represents one 'ten', so the total for the line is 100. There are white buttons on the bottom line and each one represents one 'hundred'. The total for this line is 1,000.

<u>You will need</u>

2 strips of smooth wood 1cm thick, 2cm wide and 19cm long

1 piece of smooth wood 3cm thick, 4cm wide and 20cm long

30 buttons or beads (10 black, 10 grey and 10 white)

4 nails 25mm long (brad nails, which have small heads, are ideal)

Thread or fuse wire

Hammer

Scissors (if using thread); pliers (if using fuse wire)

Knife or small hacksaw

<u>What to do</u>

1 Cut notches in the two 19cm strips of wood as shown in Fig 1. (Perhaps an adult would help you do this, as sharp knives and saws can be dangerous.)

2 Nail the strips to the large piece of wood (Fig 2), one at each end.

3 Tie the thread or wire around one of the upright strips at the bottom notch. Put 10 white buttons onto the thread or wire and tie it tightly around the notch on the opposite upright strip. Make sure the thread or wire is tight.

4 Repeat Step 3 for both the middle row and the top row, putting grey buttons onto the middle row and black ones onto the top row.

You are now ready to use your home-made abacus. It can be used to work out many different sums, by pushing the buttons one way to add and the other to subtract.

For instance, if you pushed 5 black buttons, 2 grey buttons and 1 white button to the left-hand side of the frame, what number does this represent?

Answer: 1 thousand 2 tens 5 units = 1,025

Can you work out what the highest number is that you could count on this abacus?

Answer: 1,110

Fig 1

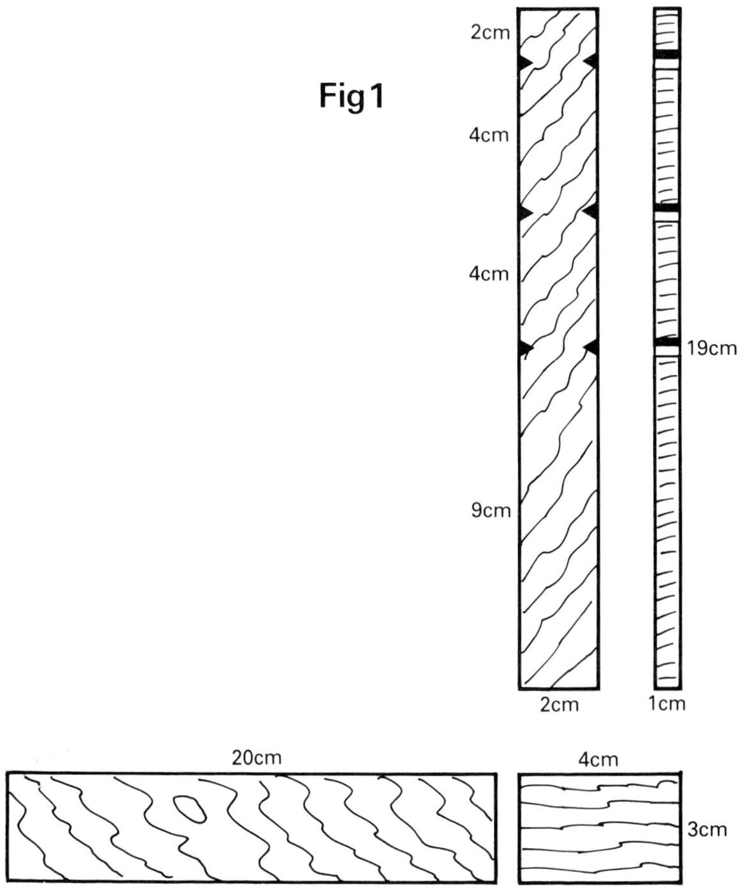

2cm

4cm

4cm

9cm

19cm

2cm

1cm

20cm

4cm

3cm

Fig 2

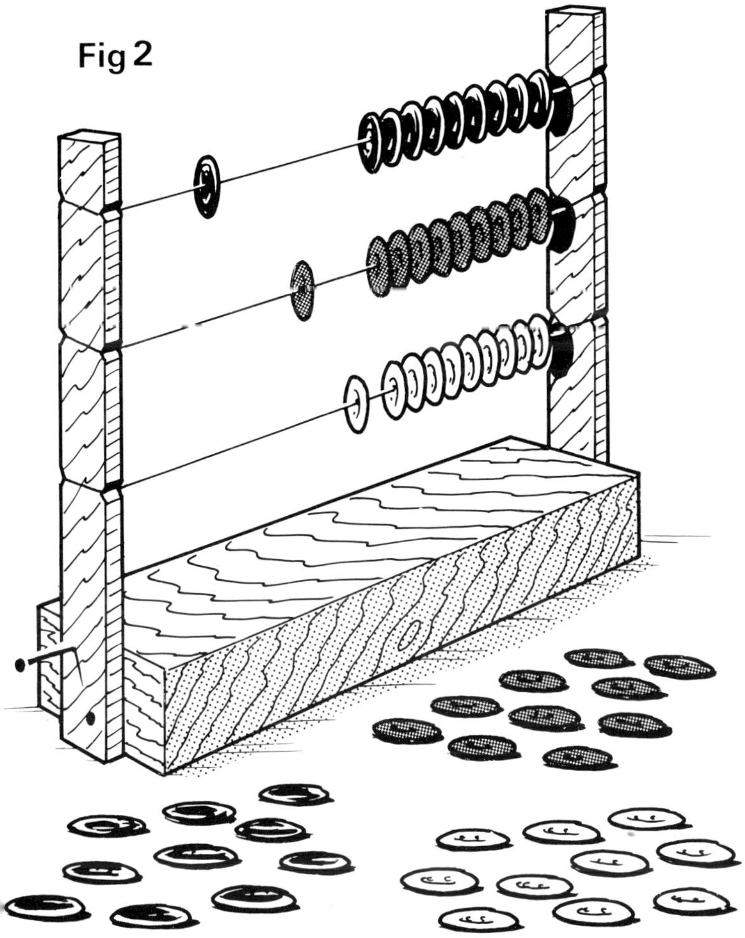

WHAT IS A COMPUTER PROGRAM?

A computer program is a set of instructions given to a computer. The word program should not be confused with the other type of programme, such as a television programme, which has a different spelling.

Through a program you instruct the computer how to use the information it has stored in its memory.

Making a computer program is almost as complicated as putting the information into the computer in the first place.

Very simply, the program tells the computer to either carry on searching or stop searching for information on all the aspects in its memory. (Remember a computer can search for half a million topics or questions in one second!)

To help them produce these programs, highly-trained people, called programmers, use special codes, called computer languages.

can be used to find answers for the same problems that only 20 years ago were being worked out by huge computers. In fact ENIAC, the first electronic computer, was 20 million times larger than a micro-chip.

It is little wonder that these tiny squares or chips are called mighty micros. Some chips are used to do calculating or working out and these are called micro-processors. Other chips can be used to store information and are called memory chips. So, in a pocket calculator, for example, you will find a micro-processor chip which calculates and a memory chip which remembers numbers. Micro-processor chips also control things, which, as we will see later, is very important. When we join the two functions together on one chip we have what is called a single-chip computer or micro-computer.

But, how can something so small (and micro is another word for small) deal with so much information? It is all to do with the 'language' a computer uses. When we give instructions to a computer, we cannot just speak to it to tell it what to do. Instead we have to use a 'language' that the computer understands. The set of instructions we give a computer is called a program. When the computer has an answer to the problem it was given or some information to give us, this language is changed into words and numbers we can read and understand.

All the computers we talk about today are micro-computers. When we join them together they become very powerful indeed. No doubt micro-chips will enable computers to get smaller and smaller. However everyday computers will not get smaller than our fingers can handle.

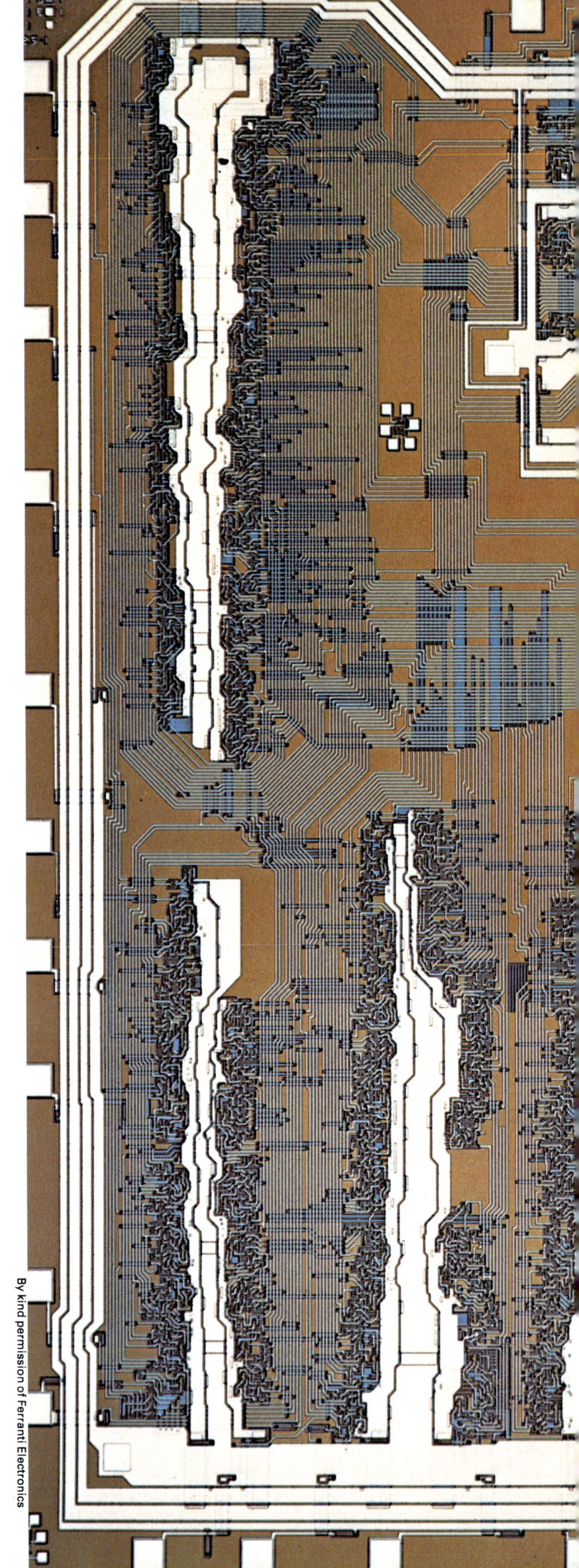

By kind permission of Ferranti Electronics

A chip showing the complicated circuit. The picture has been enlarged many times because the actual chip is only about 6mm square. This particular chip is a micro-processor. When the circuit was first made it would have been the size of the wall of a room.

FERRANTI
F101-L

From Dreams To Machines

What do you think the world will be like when you grow up? What differences will you see in the year 2000? Will we be able to transport ourselves from one planet to another, like Captain Kirk or Mr Spock of Star Trek? Will there be robots like C-3PO and R2-D2 of Star Wars to help us? Shall we be going to the Moon for holidays instead of the seaside? Or will the world be much the same as it is now?

It is not easy to answer these questions, to imagine what the future will be like. Years ago, if your parents and grandparents had been asked what the world was going to be like now, they too would have found it difficult to answer.

Very few people could have imagined the world as it is now. A fast-moving, quickly-changing, hurry-up world. A quick-as-you-can world, which is changing faster than ever before.

Hundreds of years ago things did not seem to change at all. Towns and cities stayed and looked the same from one year to another. People did not travel much – there were no cars, trains, motor-bikes or even bicycles.

Most people stayed where they were, rarely moving from where they were born, often living in the same houses that their fathers and grandfathers had lived in. Life was slower, there were not as many people in the world and, because there were no newspapers, radio or television, people in one part of the country did not know what was happening at the other end of their country. They certainly had no idea what was happening on the other side of the world. For example, news of a volcano erupting in America would probably never reach Britain.

It is difficult to imagine what life was like a few hundred years ago. Apart from no television and radio, there were very few books – and even fewer people who could read. Many of the things we now think of as being part of everyday, normal life did not exist.

There were no telephones, post, aeroplanes; no fast food like hamburgers, hot dogs or fried chicken. There weren't even ball-point or felt-tip pens! Little wonder people were not worried about the future. Life was usually the same from when you were young until you were old.

Nowadays, we have to think of the future. Changes are taking place so fast. This means that the world will without doubt be a very different place by the time you grow up.

Computers, large and small, are helping to make changes take place more quickly. Suppose someone has an idea for a new kind of car, one with a different shape. The car could be drawn on a special type of computer screen and then 'tested' on the computer. If it passes all the tests, one might be built, and in a short time, perhaps only a few years, the car might be seen on the roads.

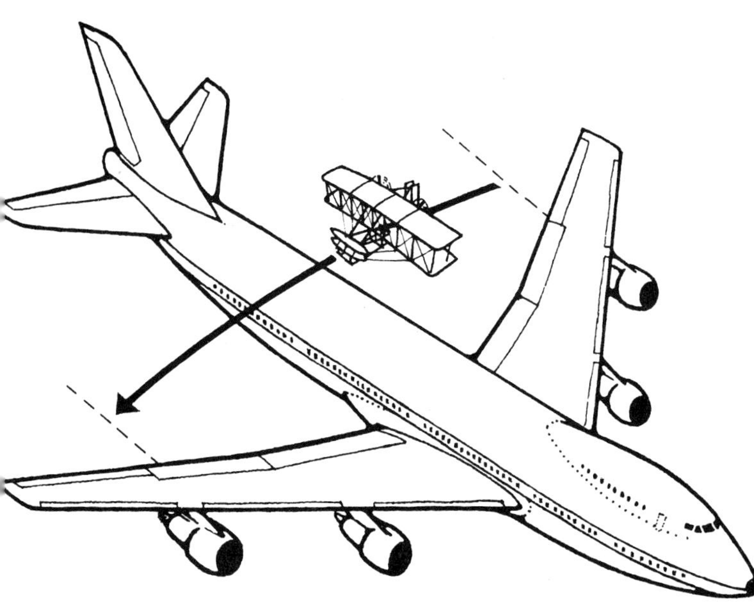

Flyer 1, which was the first plane to fly by motor power, flew a total of 36.5m which is less than the wing span of a Jumbo jet (59.64m) on 17 December 1903.

This is what makes our lifetime so exciting. Before now, it could take hundreds of years until someone's ideas or dreams became real. For example, one of the first men to imagine that one day we would be able to fly through the air in aeroplanes was Roger Bacon, an Englishman who was born in 1214.

One day, while watching builders working on the roof of a huge, new cathedral, he suddenly thought that sometime in the future machines would be able to take men from one part of the country to another. Of course, no-one believed him and he died in 1292 with only a dream of the future.

Most people forgot about Roger Bacon's idea and carried on with living from day to day. But, as we all know, the idea was eventually taken up again nearly 700 years later by two brothers, Wilbur and Orville Wright from Carolina, USA. In December 1903 the first plane in the history of man flew for only a few metres, less than the wingspan of a modern Jumbo jet. The flight lasted only 12 seconds – less time than it takes you to dial a telephone number.

At about the same time, that is in 1903, books were being written which told of men flying into space. H G Wells wrote a story called The First Men On The Moon and a book, The War In The Air. He saw the way things would go, but everyone thought it would take hundreds of years before the first space ship would leave the Earth. Even if it was possible to get a man to the Moon, surely it would be impossible to bring him back?

Man's progress towards the computer age has been very slow.

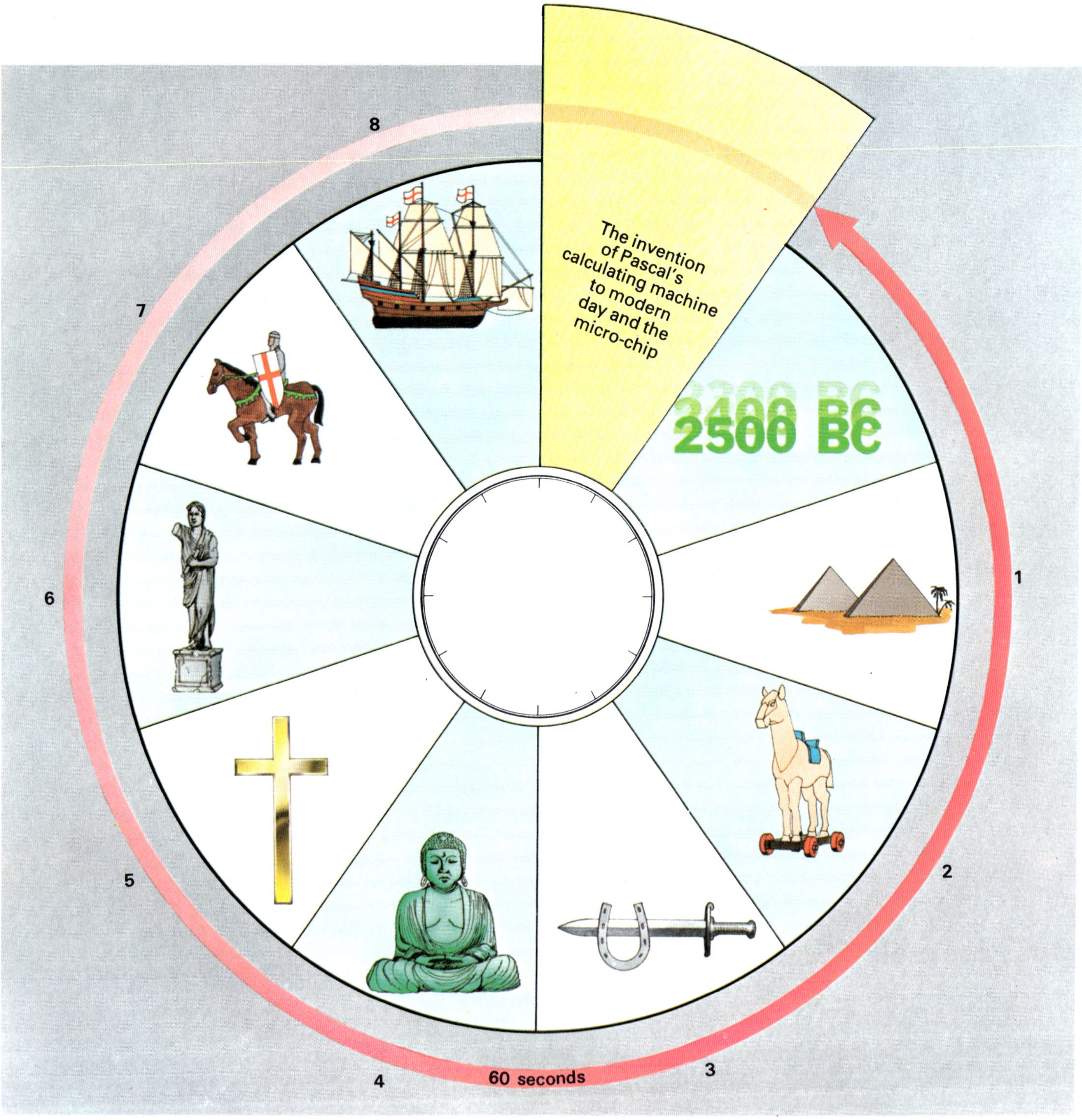

8

The invention of Pascal's calculating machine to modern day and the micro-chip

7

2400 BC

2500 BC

1

6

2

5

4

60 seconds

3

◀ Just suppose that life on Earth began with a Big Bang and all of history equalled one full year. This clock represents the last minute in the last hour of the last day of the year. The yellow segment represents the first seconds of the New Year. Look what has happened.

1 Building of the great pyramids

2 Trojan Wars

3 Discovery and use of iron

4 Birth of Buddhism

5 Birth of Christianity

6 Fall of the Roman Empire

7 Holy Crusades

8 Explorations of Sir Walter Raleigh in the Golden Hind

▶ On 21 July 1969 American astronauts, Neil Armstrong and Edwin Aldrin, became the first men to step onto the surface of the Moon. In the reflection of Edwin Aldrin's helmet Neil Armstrong can be seen standing outside the lunar module, Eagle.

▼ It is important to understand that the great leap forward, helped by computers, has happened only very recently in the history of Man.

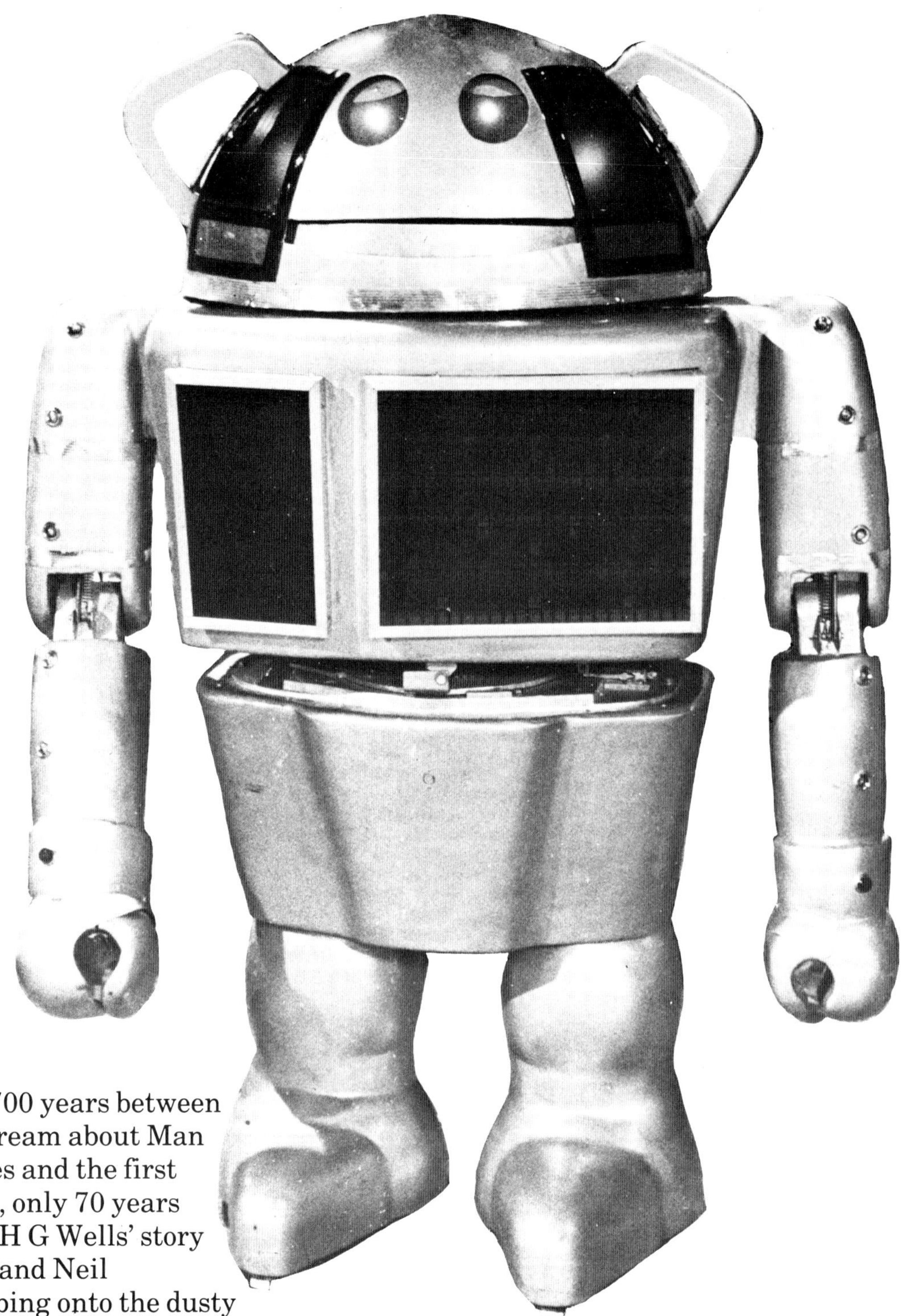
Metal Mickey

While it was 700 years between Roger Bacon's dream about Man flying aeroplanes and the first aeroplane flight, only 70 years passed between H G Wells' story about the Moon and Neil Armstrong stepping onto the dusty surface of the Moon. This is what is meant by changes taking place much faster.

The writers of Flash Gordon saw Man living in huge cities in the sky. This has not happened yet, of course. But Flash Gordon was able to talk to his friends on a telephone with a screen. Now we have an invention called a videophone on which you can see the person to whom you are talking.

If the writers of the past were right about some of the ways they saw our world changing, what about the writers of today? What do they see happening in the future?

The Metro production line, seen here, is operated by real robots. As you can see they look nothing like the normal idea of a robot as seen on television or at the cinema. Robots will only be able to do what they are told, that is to say they follow a prearranged program. Robots of the future will look like the Metro robots and it is unlikely we will see them looking like Metal Mickey.

In the television series, Star Trek, Captain Kirk and his crew are beamed down from their space ship, Enterprise, to wherever they want to go. This sort of travel really does seem to be too much to hope for and probably will not happen.

But in the film, 2001 we see people travelling to the Moon on a space bus. This is nearer the truth. Scientists are now working on, and building, a space shuttle, a sort of space truck which can carry materials as well as people into space. This means that by the time you have children of your own, you may be taking them for a holiday to the Moon and back!

What about the robots in Star Wars – C-3P0 and R2-D2? Shall we be seeing them walking around in the near future? Well, we have robots now, but not like this famous pair and we are not likely to see these fantasy robots in the future. Robots, as we know them, look nothing like human beings, but are complicated pieces of machinery which do dangerous, dirty or boring jobs. We have robots which can build cars, spray paint and go to the bottom of the sea to check oil pipes.

Again in the film, 2001, there is a computer called HAL. He is a special computer, as he can speak like a human and play games like chess. Far-fetched? Absolutely impossible? Not at all. In most big stores you can buy a hand-held machine that 'speaks' to you, giving you words to spell. As you tap the letters it repeats them and lets you know if you are right or wrong. There are also chess computers, which look like ordinary chess boards. But these are very different because they are programmed to challenge you by working out moves. Some of these chess computers can beat the best players in the world.

So we may be able to get some clues about the future from the writers of today. But one thing no writer of the past imagined was the invention of the micro-chip, which we looked at in the last chapter. It is the micro-chip which will help speed up the changes to come.

Many of the things we see and use as part of our everyday life could be different. Television, for example, will become something more than family entertainment. By joining up a television to a computer we will be able to switch into a wonderful world of information. For example, we will be able to find out when trains are running, the latest news and even how to mend a puncture. This is something which is beginning to happen now in Britain.

As you will see in the following pages, the micro-chip is going to make a great difference to our way of life in the future, not only in the home, but at school, at work and at play.

By kind permission of British Leyland

THE CHANGING FACE OF OUR WORLD

If you looked quickly at the two pictures on these pages, you might think they showed two completely different places. But, if you look carefully, you will see that both pictures have some identical features and are, in fact, pictures of the same place, but years apart.

The top picture is a view of typical British countryside about three hundred years ago. The one below it is the same view but set in the year 1981.

Which features occur in both pictures? There is the church which hasn't altered in three hundred years and there's the old manor house by the river. The horizon, too, hasn't changed.

A lot has altered, of course. Look carefully and see where the changes have occurred.

What will this same scene be like in one hundred years time – in the year 2181? Much will have happened between now and then. Some things will probably stay the same. Few people would want to pull down a lovely, old manor house, for example. But will the airport still be there and will cars still be travelling along the motorway?

Why not take a piece of tracing paper? Carefully trace the outline of the horizon from the bottom picture. The horizon is the line where the sky meets the ground. Add certain features such as the river and . . . What features do you think will stay almost or just the same? What major changes will have happened by 2181 and what will they look like?

Learning For The Future

You go to a school to learn. Your father and mother went to a school to learn. Although home and school are different places, we can also learn a lot in our homes. In the past school has helped us to learn certain things more quickly by going out of our homes and meeting together in a school. In the future we may find that more and more learning is done at home as well as at school.

Firstly we should look at how schools developed before we move on to what schools might be in the future. Hundreds of years ago, very few children had the chance of going to a school. Most youngsters, from the ages of six and seven onwards, were sent to work in fields and down coal mines and, a little later on, in horrible factories. They worked long and hard for little money. They could not read or write and the only 'teaching' they were given was through Scripture readings and saying prayers in workhouses, places where the very poor lived.

Those lucky enough to be born rich went to grammar schools, usually run by the Church, where they learned Greek, Latin and English grammar, as well as some mathematics. The most important book then was thought to be the

A village school in 1840. Unlike modern classrooms, there are no desks and children of different ages are being taught by one teacher.

Bible and the stories the children were told were of heroes who had lived thousands of years before in Rome and Greece.

About 150 years ago, as the world began to change and more people moved into towns and cities, a few charity schools and Sunday schools were opened for the poor who could not afford the cost of grammar schools. But it was not until 1870, just over 100 years ago, that the government decided every child had to go to school.

The new schools taught science, mathematics, book-keeping (a way of keeping records) and, of course, reading and writing as well as religious instruction. Grammar schools kept on with Latin and Greek, but they too had to teach their pupils other subjects.

The idea was that every child should have five hours teaching a day, five days a week. Now, over 100 years later, that is still how you are meant to be taught. The trouble was, in the early days of schools, many parents thought the government had no right to make their children go to school. They preferred to send their children out to work long hours in shops and factories which left very little time for learning. It was difficult to keep children at school because parents needed the money their children could earn. It was hoped children would stay at school until they were 15 years old, but in fact many left when they were 11 or 12 to go to work. Nowadays, of course, the leaving age is 16, and many older children want to stay on even longer to learn more.

Before we peep into the future, let's think about what we mean by learning. We start learning the moment we are born. We learn things like walking and even talking and later we learn different things like how to cross the road, how to eat with knives and forks and how to tie our shoelaces.

During our first years at school we learn to read, count and write. If we didn't learn to do these three things it would be difficult, if not impossible, to learn other subjects. You can say that reading, writing and mathematics are the diving boards from which you can jump into a huge pool of knowledge.

The boy and girl are using a computer linked to a television set. This sort of apparatus should become very common in the school of the future. The flat terminal on the right has an electronic pencil on it. A careful drawing can be made on the terminal, which the computer can read. The drawing is then flashed onto the television screen.

As we get older we continue to learn – how to ride a bike or even, later on, drive a car. Grown-ups learn how to do their jobs. In fact really we never stop learning. What we are doing is picking up lots of little bits of information and we call all this information knowledge.

The knowledge we gather comes from many different sources. At school the teacher tells us things that increase our knowledge of different subjects, say history and French. Newspapers, radio, television and magazines give us more knowledge, say about football or politicians. We find out what is happening in the world by listening to and watching the news. We can discover fascinating facts about Nature, from radio and television, as well as books and magazines. But no-one would say that a newspaper, a radio or a television set was the same as a teacher. We cannot ask a newspaper a question, for example. A radio or a book does not know when you have made a mistake and cannot tell you where you have gone wrong. You cannot tell a normal television programme to slow down, because you did not understand the last point being made. (Well, you can tell it, but it would do you no good!) Knowledge comes from your television set to you. You have no control over what programmes are on the set. Until not so long ago, all you could do was sit in front of a television and watch.

But a few years ago that changed. It became possible to use televisions for more than just watching shows, films or cartoons. Shops began to sell games which could be played on your television screens, like Space Invaders, tennis, car races and football. These are electronic games. The special box has links which go into your television set and when you press certain buttons and levers different games appear on the television screen. The very important point here is that *you* control what happens on the television screen.

How do they work? The boxes have micro-chips in them which means they are small computers. The micro-chips will enable various games, such as Space Invaders or football, to be played on your television screen. However, putting Space Invaders on your screen is only one of the many things such a micro-computer could do. For example, certain micro-computers could put the whole of the history of British kings and queens on your screen.

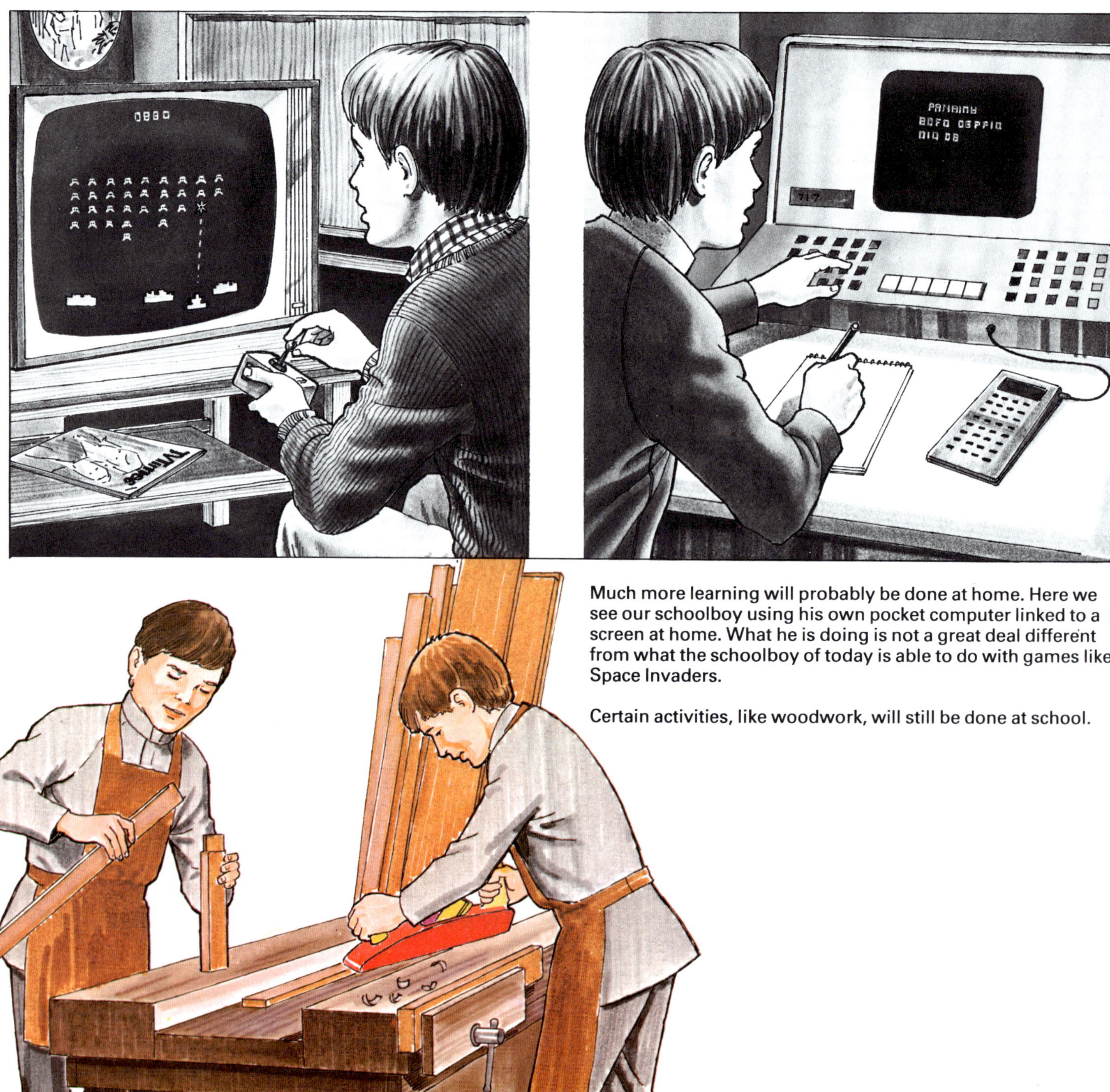

Much more learning will probably be done at home. Here we see our schoolboy using his own pocket computer linked to a screen at home. What he is doing is not a great deal different from what the schoolboy of today is able to do with games like Space Invaders.

Certain activities, like woodwork, will still be done at school.

Schools might become more like community centres and less like buildings with classrooms in. Adults will have more free time and will probably spend time with their children and other adults at school. Notice the boy is carrying his pocket computer with him. This can be linked to screens at school.

As we have already seen, micro-chips can be used to store huge amounts of information. If we can control what we look at, as with the electronic games, then it is clear that we can also control vast amounts of information to be replayed on the screen that we can look at and listen to.

Such computers as we have been describing, including the electronic games, could change our whole way of learning in the future.

In the future, when your children are beginning to learn, there could be teaching computers in use all over the country. These teaching computers will not be machines that look like humans and they won't be standing in front of a class of children giving lessons. They are more likely to be computers which have been programmed to recognise you and they will go only as fast as each of you can understand. It will be like having your very own teacher always near at hand.

These computers may well be very small and each person will have his or her own computer which could be about the size of a pocket calculator today. These could be carried around and connected to a larger screen when needed.

However, do not get confused between a teaching computer and a calculator. The computer will be able to understand letters and possibly even your voice. Most pocket calculators today only use numbers, not letters. The teaching computer will probably include dictionaries for English and foreign languages and they will be able to let you know if you are making mistakes.

You probably will not be able to obtain every film to show on your home video. A school could be the place to go to in order to see a new or very expensive film, perhaps about the fastest-ever ascent of Mount Everest.

But for the young children who are beginning to learn to read, write and count, the first teaching computers might well be found in their own homes for it is possible that children will not be going to school at such an early age in the future.

Some people think that in the future young children will be put into groups of four or five, all living close to one another, who will be taught by a 'granny' or 'grandad', who is really a kind of teacher. All the first steps of learning could come from the computer. All the children could take part in the lessons by using a keyboard to show their answers or a light pencil to make drawings.

Does all this mean that there will be no more schools? No, it does not, but schools might be different from the way they are today. They could become places where you go to relax, meet friends and play sports on the recreation fields, swim in the swimming pool and borrow books and cassettes from the library. Of course, at the moment many schools already have these facilities, but perhaps in the future, adults, as well as children, will be able to go to school to enjoy them.

You may not want to buy a film cassette, in which case you could always go along to the school library to borrow some, just as you can borrow books at the moment.

Children will play games together at school, just as they do now. Perhaps adults too will be able to go along for a game of tennis or some other sport.

The latest electronic games might also be available in these schools for you and your family to borrow, just like you borrow books from the library now.

Schools like this will also be places to learn, just as they are now. But, again, adults will be learning as well as children, because in our changing world there is so much to learn even when we grow up.

At the moment many grown-ups go to night school and training courses to learn, but in future many more people will be learning with the help of all the equipment that the micro-chip will make available. Perhaps Mum will go to school to learn about computers and how to program them and Dad will go to learn about writing music.

We will still be learning, as we learn today, but computers, both at home and in school, will help us to acquire knowledge and skills needed to live in our quickly changing world.

A House As Big As The Universe

Thanks to micro-chips life in the future could be more comfortable, easier and more fun. A visit to a house of the future will show you how this could be. From the outside, houses will seem much the same. But inside, there is a world of difference. Let's imagine what a house in the future might be like.

The changes begin at the front door. You will not find a keyhole. Instead there is a small panel at the side of the door. Inside the panel is a micro-chip, which is connected to the door lock. The door will open only if the micro-chip recognises your voice or the voices of the other people living in the house. To make sure, you may have to put your fingers on the panel, to allow the chip to identify your fingerprints. So there is less chance of burglars in our house of the future!

Inside the house you may come across a small home robot which is sweeping the carpet. The back garden is being mowed by another robot with a lawn mower built into it. You will notice that the house is not too warm and not too cold, in fact it is just right. This is because every room has a temperature control unit fitted with a micro-chip on the wall.

The front room, or lounge, has a few chairs in it and in one corner there is a video recorder, to record television programmes or show the latest films borrowed from the library or bought from a shop. There is also a video disc machine, which is very like a record player, but instead of only sound, you also have pictures.

All the machines we use for our pleasure and enjoyment, such as recorders, record players and disc machines, will be smaller, about the size of a thick paperback book. They will not need to be large, because the cassettes, records and discs will be smaller. In fact, you will be able to have a film like Star Wars in a cassette the size of a matchbox.

If you feel like watching television, you can sit down in front of what looks like a wide, flat, silvery board on the wall. This is a television of the future which hangs like a painting with the screen as large as you wish it to be. But what will you watch? The answer to that question is practically anything from around the world.

At the moment in Britain there are not many different television channels from which to choose. When you grow up, you will be able to choose from many different channels. These will come from different countries and will be beamed to your home from satellites circling the Earth. Special aerials, called dish aerials, will pick up signals from the satellites. If you tune into a programme from France, a micro-chip inside your television will change the language into English. You will not have to hold a huge remote control with hundreds of buttons on it, because your television, hi-fi and other electronic machines will all work by voice control. All you have to do is ask the television to change channels and it will. So there is no chance of pressing the wrong button!

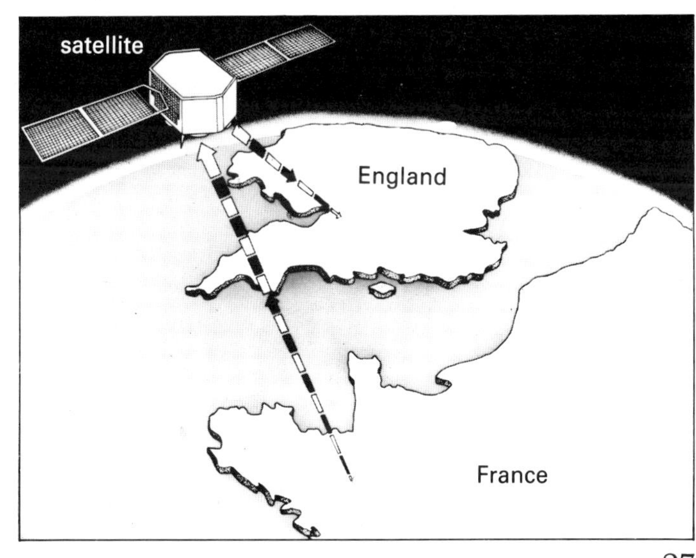

The satellites, which will be going around the Earth, will not only be able to bring you more television programmes. They are going to mean the end of telephones as we know them. You will be able to talk to friends, or people you work with, through wrist communicators. These will look a little like digital watches and will still be able to tell you the time. But they are also very powerful radio telephones. Inside, once again, is a micro-chip and all you will have to do is speak into them. Touch a button and you will hear your friend's answer.

What is happening is that your wrist communicator is sending out signals to the satellite high above the Earth, which then beams down your message to one on your friend's wrist. It will not matter where you are in the world. You could be sitting on a sunny beach in Spain and still be able to talk to a friend in Scotland!

This is what we expect to happen; but back to our imaginary house. You may not feel like watching television or a film. You may choose to plug one of your many video games into the television set. These games will probably be in the same room as the television and hi-fi, which is why this room may become known as an entertainment room, a place where you can rest and play.

You will probably have another room, known as a study, where your newspaper comes in and is printed and where you will keep your home computer. The computer, which looks like a large desk with a television on it, is another link with the world. Every morning you can find out what is happening by turning on the news. On your screen you will see the main stories and if you want to find out more about a story, say a football match, for example, all you have to do is ask. If you want to keep the news story, a small printer at the side of the screen will print you a sheet with the news on it.

Here we see four rooms from our possible house of the future. Micro-chip technology will mean great advances in many forms of home equipment and, for those who can afford these, life will become more comfortable.

AS
RCW
MCW
13:00

Mrs Smith checks her home computer to see what shopping she needs.

She then links directly with the supermarket general computer and makes her order.

Mrs Smith could order all her shopping over the home computer and have it delivered to her door. Otherwise she could go and do her own shopping.

Your computer will be linked to other computers, which means certain people would be able to do most of their work from home. As you will see later, the type of work you may be doing will probably be different from the work we do now. But having computers linked will also mean that your own terminal (the correct name for your computer) is a learning machine. So the study will be where most of the family's learning will take place. We must remember that these other computers, as well as your own, will have huge memories. You will probably be able to find out anything you need from your home computer. It will be like having the biggest library in the world in your own house.

Let's move to the kitchen and imagine what changes could have taken place there. There will still be an oven, of course, but with a difference. The oven of the future has a micro-chip built into its controls. This could mean that everyone in the family will be able to have his or her food cooked just the way they like it. If Dad likes crispy bacon and you don't, the tiny computer in the oven will make sure that the bacon on the top level is crisp, while that below is not. The memory in the micro-chip can be programmed to remember how everyone likes his or her food.

The accountant's terminal at the supermarket works out the bill and checks her account at the bank.

Supermarkets will probably be similar to today's, except that the tills will rarely see cash and should be very quick. The computer terminal at the cash desk recognises the EAN coding and prices each article.

The EAN system (**E**uropean **A**rticle **N**umbering). Every product in each size, colour, flavour and pack is given an identifying number. The computer recognises the arrangement of black and white lines.

The micro-chip in the oven, as well as the micro-chips throughout the rest of the house, are all connected to a central computer. All you have to do is tell the computer when you want to eat and the oven will take care of the rest! The cooker could even send out a signal to your wrist communicator when your dinner is ready and from it a small voice will come to let you know. If, by any chance, you are not ready to eat, there is no chance of the food being spoiled. The micro-chip will put the oven on a 'hold-over', keeping the food warm.

Where else will you find our friend the micro-chip? In the fridge and in the freezer, for a start. Should the amount of food you have in them run low, you will be told. As you open the door of the fridge or the freezer, a voice will let you know you are running out of food! This means, of course, that you will have to buy more food. But, again, this is no problem for the shopper of the future. No-one really likes going to a crowded supermarket and waiting in long queues to pay. In the future this need not happen. All you will have to do is sit at your home computer, or terminal, press a few buttons and you will be linked directly to the supermarket.

You will be able to order from the lists of goods shown on your computer screen. Special offers, discounts and so forth will all be shown and you can choose what you want and place your order directly. Your shopping will either be delivered right to your door or prepared, ready for you to collect.

What about paying? Simple. The list which flashed up on your screen came from a computer at the supermarket which also showed the cost. You will then tap out a number on the keyboard in front of the screen. This number is your bank number. By tapping out your number you will be joining up the computer at the bank with the computer in the supermarket. The bank computer will transfer the correct amount of money to the supermarket computer. Of course, no real money will pass from computer to computer. What will happen is that the cost of the shopping will be subtracted from the money you have in the bank.

Not only food will be paid for in this way. Everything you buy will be paid through a computer. You will be able to choose almost anything from a new car to a toy while sitting in your chair. To pay, all you will do is let the computer at your bank know. It will do the rest. If you are not at home, you will be able to use a credit card, a small plastic card, which will have your bank number, name and address on it.

What all this is going to mean is that there will be no need to carry lots of money about, which should make life safer for most of us. Even if someone manages to steal your card, it won't be of any use. Your card can only be used by you. This is because the computer at the bank will know who you are and will recognise either your voice or your fingerprints. Apart from this, you will have a secret code, which you alone will know.

But, to come back to our kitchen of the future. You will see a small screen on one of the counters. This is not only a television but a cook book as well. A small cassette or disc will be slipped under the screen and you are not only told what you need to make, for instance, a cake, but actually shown how to do it.

In the home of the future, micro-chips will be working from morning to night. In the morning, they will make sure your coffee is ready, open your curtains and have a paper ready for you. During the day they will keep the house warm or cool, depending on the weather outside.

At night, they will ensure all the lights are off and the doors locked. They will do everything you ask, just like the genie in Aladdin's lamp.

Micro-chips should make life easier for us in the future. They will make sure we are wasting less lighting and heating, which will save money and energy. You may be worried about being able to afford all these micro-computers in your home. But by the time you grow up micro-chips will probably be cheaper than what you are paying now for an ice-cream.

So, your home will no longer end where the walls end, because you will be able to link up with other computers. In many ways your home will become as big as the world itself. Or, perhaps, even as big as the Universe!

We can see that banks, shops, offices and homes will all have direct links with each other. Money business can be handled very quickly and if paper records are needed, statements can be provided through the teleprinter to offices or homes.

The EAN system makes keeping records and stock-taking much easier. Goods can be re-ordered from the warehouse and brought by van to the loading bay. A customer's goods could be delivered by a battery-operated three-wheel vehicle.

MAKE YOUR OWN INFORMATION SELECTOR

Master card 14cm

1½cm

Red Yellow Orange Blue Green Brown Purple Black

9cm

ORANGE

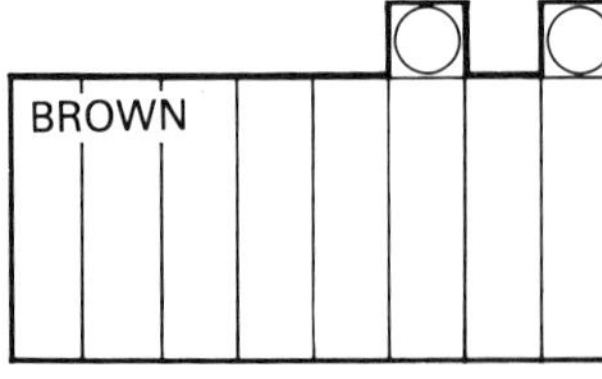

RED

BLUE

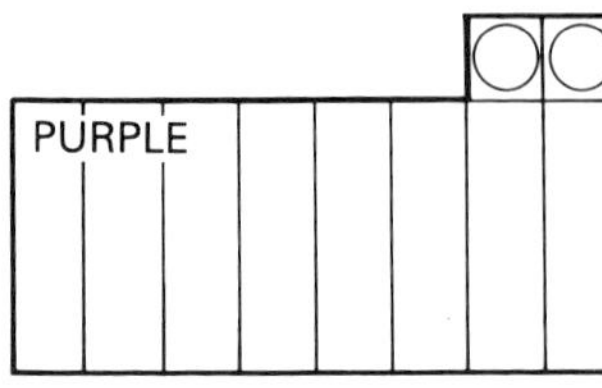

All computers store vast amounts of information. What makes them so useful to us is not just the amount of information they hold, but the speed at which the computers can select what you need.

Here we can make our own simple information selector. Through this we shall see that by a simple process answers can be gained to various questions.

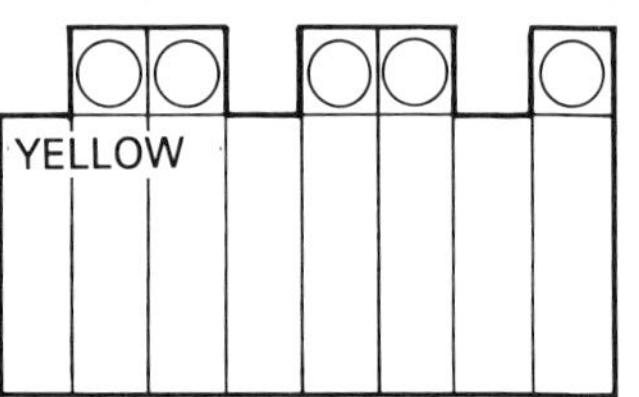

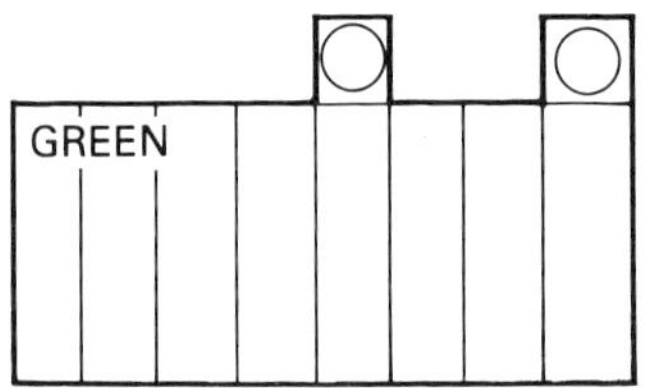

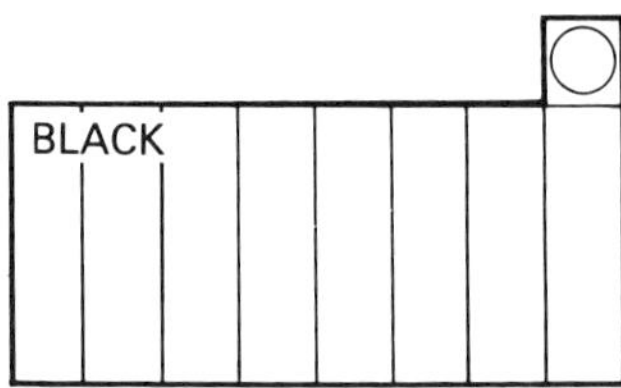

A computer does not operate through holes and needles, of course, but through special circuits, as we have seen earlier.

This information selector is like a computer because it can give you answers to a certain set of questions. But first you must give it all the information it needs.

This information selector is made up of nine cards. Each card should be 14cm by 9cm (the size of an average postcard).

Follow these steps:

1 Rule a line across the card 1½cm down from the top on each card.

2 Draw dividing lines to give you eight equal sections 17.5mm apart on each card.

3 The master card will need holes punched in every section above the top line.

4 Take a card for each of the eight colours and mark it with one colour – orange or brown or red, etc. Follow the cards shown.

5 Very carefully and neatly punch in the holes as shown on the colour cards.

6 Cut out the sections above the ruled line that don't have holes punched in.

7 Finally, mark the master card with all the colours in the order shown. It is important that you follow the order: 1-red, 2-yellow, 3-orange, 4-blue, 5-green, 6-brown, 7-purple, 8-black.

8 Pack the cards neatly together with the master card on top.

What we can find out

If you want to know what colours make up other colours, orange for example, stand the pack on its side facing you and push a knitting needle or thin pencil through the hole marked orange. Carefully separate the cards attached to the needle from those left behind.

You will be left with the master card, the card marked orange and those marked red and yellow. Therefore, red and yellow together make orange.

Carefully try all the holes and see what happens.

Some colours are called primary colours and are not made up from other colours. Can you find them?

One colour is made up of all the other colours put together. Can you find it?

Work Time, Play Time

By kind permission of Massey Ferguson Ltd

In the days before machinery was easily available, men and women worked on the land using hand tools, such as scythes for cutting corn. Now highly mechanised combine harvesters are used to do the same work more quickly and efficiently.

A few hundred years ago you would have had little or no choice about what kind of work you would do when you grew up. If you were a boy, you would probably do what your father did and girls would do the same as their mothers. So most boys would work on farms and most girls would look after the home and children.

The world was different in those days. There were far fewer towns and cities. Most people lived in the country, growing and harvesting food. All the work was done by hand. We only had muscles to help us then, either our own muscles or those of animals. At harvest time all the crops had to be gathered by hand and taken to markets in nearby towns in carts pulled by horses. Wheat had to be cut with a scythe, a kind of curved knife, bundled together and taken to the mill for grinding into flour. The flour would then be taken to a baker to be made into bread.

A lot of people had to work very hard to make sure there were enough loaves of bread. Someone had to cut the wheat, another person had to collect it and tie it into bundles, someone else had to take it to the mill and another person to the baker. So in those days people worked on the land to keep everyone fed. In fact, out of every 100 people who worked, 92 of them worked on farms. These 92 people were needed to make sure that they and the other eight had enough food.

Nowadays it is different. Out of every 100 people working in Britain today only two work on farms to keep the other 98 fed. This is because farmers now have machines to help them, like combine harvesters, tractors and spraying machines. These machines became the tools a farmer could use instead of his hands and muscles. The first machines, or tools, used steam to power them and tractors with steam engines could be seen on the land.

These machines not only did more work, they were also faster. They could do all the work in one day that before had taken 10 men. Because they were faster, the farmers had some spare time to do other things. They began to find out more about growing crops and, as they learnt more, they grew more and better crops. With these new machines doing the work of so many men, these men could find other jobs.

Other machines were being used to make many of the things we use and need, such as clothes, shoes and even other machines. These machines were big and had to be put into large buildings in or around towns. These large buildings were called factories.

The men and women in the country, who no longer worked on the land, began moving into the towns and cities to work in these factories. All this took place about 150 years ago. So there was a move from farms to factories. Women worked with the machines and then later also helped with all the paperwork. Some became secretaries and typists.

As machines became better and faster, some of the men and women who had been working with them began to work in offices. They had to make sure that all the goods made in the factories reached the people who wanted them. Other people began to work in shops, selling many of the things that had been made in factories. It was not long before there were more people working in shops and offices than in factories. So there had been another move – from factories to offices.

Hundreds of years ago people worked from dawn until dusk. Gradually the number of hours spent working each day has been reduced. Now, in Britain for example, people work about 7 or 8 hours a day and this is likely to fall in the future.

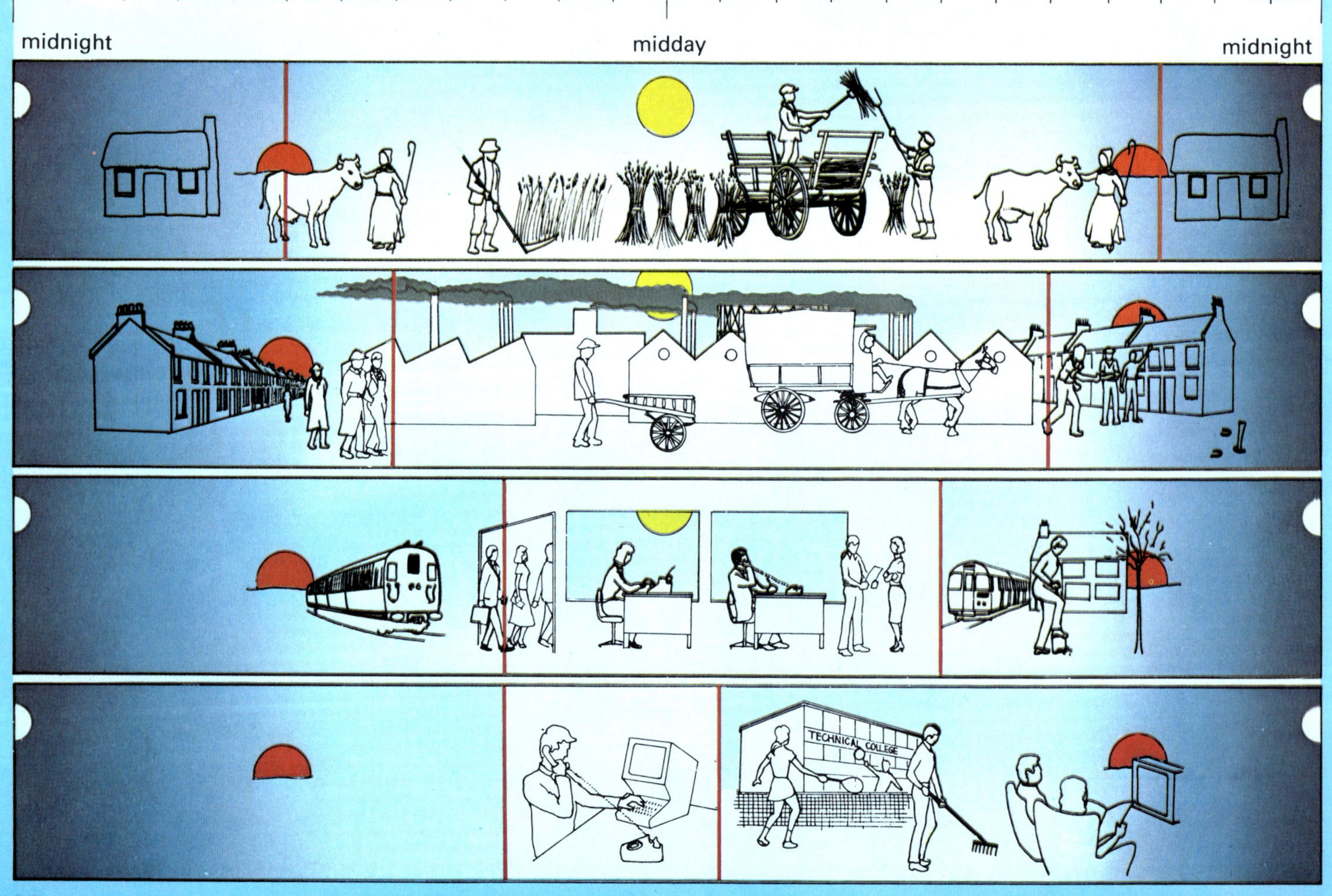

The people who work on farms are called farm workers, the people in factories are called factory workers, while those in offices and shops could be called service workers. A good example of a service is the Post Office. But why is it called a service, when not everyone is actually serving us? In fact, we are being served by people working in offices, even though we don't actually see them.

Suppose you are visiting London and want to send a postcard to a friend in Scotland. First of all, you have to buy a stamp at the Post Office. Then you put your card in a postbox, where it is collected by a postman in a van. It is then taken to a sorting office, where it is put with other letters, packages and cards going to Scotland. These are all put on a train to Scotland and when they arrive they are sorted out again and sent to different towns and cities. Then a postman delivers the card to your friend.

So, a lot of work, involving a lot of people, goes into getting letters and cards from one place to another. You only see a few of these people, such as the postman and the person behind the counter. But there are many people you do not see, who work in offices, making sure everything runs smoothly.

These men and women have to work out the best time to collect the letters, they have to know when the trains are leaving and make sure the mail is on them. There also has to be someone who knows the best type of vans to buy and someone has to decide where to put the postboxes. What these men and women are working with is information. They have to know the best ways of doing their jobs.

Knowledge has become very important. It's all part of the hurry-up world in which we are living where new discoveries are being made nearly every day. More and more people are spending their time working with this knowledge, because there is so much. They store it and use it, passing it on when anyone needs it.

One example of stored information is a telephone directory. There are thousands of names, addresses and telephone numbers in each directory. Now, with a micro-chip which can store information, it is possible to put a whole telephone directory in the memory of one micro-chip. So, in a few years you could be using a small screen linked to a micro-chip to find a telephone number. Micro-chips are already being used to store knowledge in places where it is needed, like offices, for example, where men and women work with information.

By kind permission of Hamilton Rentals Service Sales

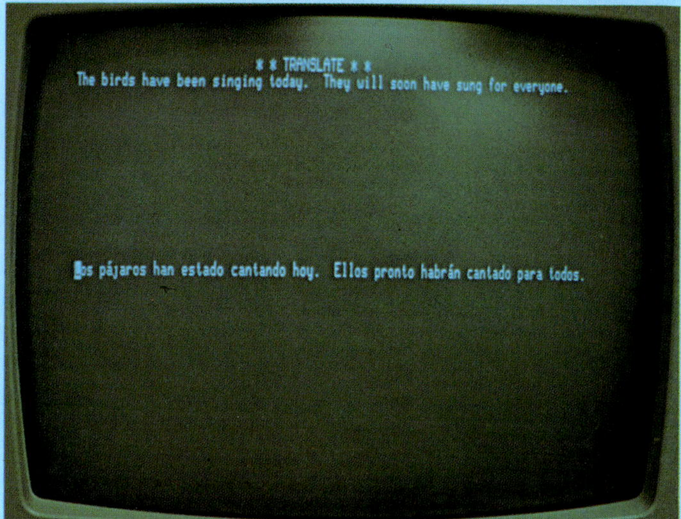

In an hour this word translator changes or translates 14,000 words from one language to another.

Micro-chips, remember, are really kinds of tiny information machines. So machines and tools with micro-chips in them can do much more than ordinary machines and tools. A typewriter, for example, with a micro-chip in it, becomes a **word processor,** not only typing letters, but making sure there are no mistakes. A machine which cuts metal to make doors for cars can have a micro-chip controlling it, which means the machine always cuts in the same way and therefore the car doors are always the right size.

Micro-chips, then, are helping to do a lot of our work in offices and factories. They do a lot of the boring and sometimes dangerous work we have had to do ourselves. Jobs like spraying

By kind permission of Rank Xerox Ltd

Computerised machinery makes office work much faster and more efficient. An office like this, with word and information processing equipment, will become common in the future. A lot of information can be stored on the floppy discs, which you can see the operator taking from the cabinet.

cars have always been dangerous because if paint is breathed in, it can make a person very ill. So now spraying machines with micro-chips built into them have taken over. The micro-chips guide and move the spray arm to make sure every part of the car is sprayed properly.

The micro-chip has information which it uses to guide the spray arm. Of course we put the information onto the micro-chip in the first place. In car factories, micro-chips have been put on many of the machines which men used to control. When a machine and micro-chip get together, the new kind of machine is called a robot. Now it is possible to build most of a car with robots. All a human being does is drive it! You may have thought a robot was something that looked like a metal human being – R2-D2, for example. Perhaps one day robots like R2-D2 will be built. But now, and for a long time to come, robots will look nothing like human beings. But they will be able to work 24 hours a day and should never make mistakes.

But what about all the people who did the jobs that robots now do? Where will all the typists and secretaries go as 'smart' typewriters do most of their work? Before trying to find answers to these questions,we need to look again at what happened before when there were other shifts in the kind of work people did.

When machines began to do some of the work on farms, the farm workers left for the towns and cities. There many of them found work in the factories. These factory workers could produce more goods in a day because they were working with machines.

In the last 100 years, the number of hours spent working has been cut in half. Men who worked 60 hours a week 100 years ago, nowadays only work 30 hours. By the time you grow up, there will be even less time spent working and more time spent doing other things.

All this started when machines began to be used on farms and then in factories. The first machines, steam engines, gave us extra muscle power and gave us time to think and discover.

The second kind of machines, the electronic machines, which were to become computers, gave us extra brain power. They allowed us to think of better ways of making the things we needed like cars, clothes, food and furniture. Just as using steam engines gave workers of the past more time, so computers will give *us* more time.

What this will mean is that not so many people will spend their worktime making things for other people. In fact, by the time you are adults, it will take only 10 people to make enough food, furniture, cars and so on, for another 90 people. What will all the people do?

They will probably be doing what many people are already beginning to do. They will be working with information. Just as new kinds of jobs were found in factories for those who came from the farms, it seems very likely that new jobs will be found working with computers.

Receiving information means knowing and knowing means learning. In the future you will be learning throughout your life. You may change your job so you will need information about each new job. Many people will be giving information to others.

There have been changes before and there will be changes again. But the changes you will see taking place are not like any the world has ever seen. For the first time, there may be no need to 'go to work'. It could become possible for you to do your work from home.

It seems very likely that the time will come when you will have much more leisure time – time for hobbies and for playing sport and, of course, for learning. You will have time to travel to countries all over the world, such as China, India and probably Russia. There will be fewer problems with understanding and speaking different languages because you will have a pocket electronic dictionary which will speak for you.

Since Man first appeared on the Earth, he has been gathering information about the world around him. Now we have more information than ever before. But there is still a lot to find out about ourselves, the world and, of course, space. So there is a lot to do, but now we have more time to do it.

FUN FACTORY

It is probable that in the future people will have much more free time to themselves. Areas likely to become even more important will be sport and recreation. Our artist has drawn a fun factory of the future and placed it on the Moon. It includes everything from indoor cricket to hang-gliding. If this seems like a far-fetched idea, just remember that Neil Armstrong stepped onto the Moon as early as 1969 and we have developed the technology to build such projects. The biggest factor, of course, holding back such a fun factory would be the enormous expense.

Your Future Health

No-one likes being ill. Even a cold can make you feel grumpy and fed up. So, thank goodness there are doctors who can help make you fit and well again. But doctors don't just wave magic wands and you're better.

Doctors have to ask you questions to find out what is wrong with you. They have to know if you have any pains. They must know how you feel and how long you have been ill. They must know if you have any spots, have been sick and many other things. What doctors are doing is gathering information about you. Then, and only then, will they tell you what kind of medicine, if any, you should take. This means that they have to know all about different medicines. To do that a doctor has to spend a lot of time finding out about them.

All these different things to be found out take time. Once the doctor has seen you, he or she has to write notes for your personal file. So if you have to visit him again, he can look up your file to remind him of what has been wrong with you in the past and which medicines you have taken.

Of course, you are not the only person the doctor has to see. Take a look at any waiting room and you will have an idea of how many people one doctor deals with. If you are too ill to go to his surgery, he has to visit you at home and this takes even more time.

Doctors are there to help us keep fit and healthy. But because they spend so much time asking questions, writing notes and driving from place to place, they don't have much time left over to spend with the people who really need them, people who are really ill. Much of their time is spent gathering information.

Now, we have already seen that computers can be used to gather information, so in the future it is very likely that doctors will be using computers to do a lot of their work for them.

There might come a time when a computer in your own home can take your temperature and blood pressure and find out where you are feeling pain. This information could then be passed to a computer in the doctor's surgery so that he can give you the correct medicine. If this happens it will save a lot of the doctor's time.

Saving time is only one way computers will help the doctors of the future. Computers will also help doctors and scientists find better ways of fighting diseases and curing many of the illnesses we now know little about. It is possible that by the time you are old, cures will have been found for most of the diseases which now kill people.

As we have seen, micro-chips are helping to make machines and computers smaller and this means that medical equipment will be easy to fit into a smaller area. Ambulances of the future could be much better equipped than they are at present, with the result that the lives of many people will be saved through immediate treatment.

But perhaps the most exciting change you will see will be the replacement of bad and faulty parts of our bodies by brand new limbs, like arms and legs, and organs, like lungs and hearts. Doctors have always learnt from Nature, but only now are we beginning to understand some of Nature's secrets.

For example, a salamander, a kind of newt, doesn't worry too much if it loses a leg. It simply grows another one. It can only do this, though, during the first stage of its life, when it cannot yet live on dry land, but has to spend all its time in the water. When we lose an arm or leg, we are not able to grow new ones. We have to make them. The Bionic Man had special arms and legs made which turned out to be better than the ones he lost! But, up until very recently, artificial limbs, made of plastic and metal, have not been able to do what normal arms and legs do.

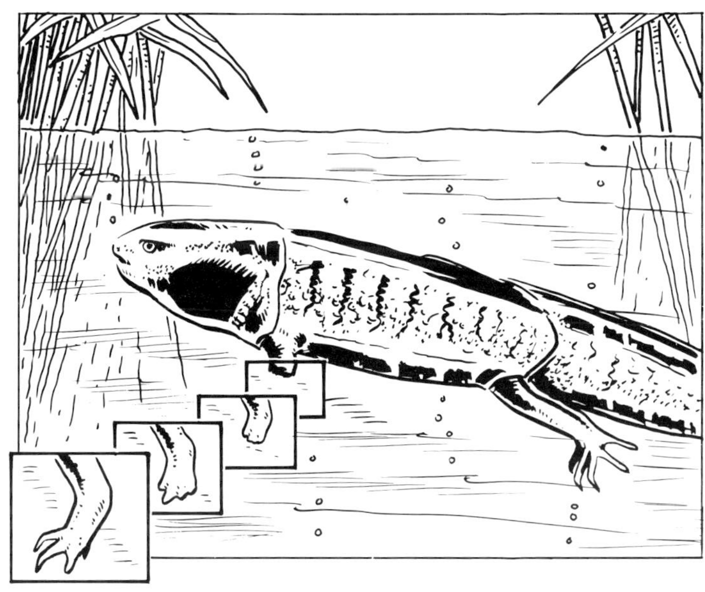

▲ During the first stage of a salamander's life it can only live in the water. If it loses a limb during this time a new one is gradually regrown.

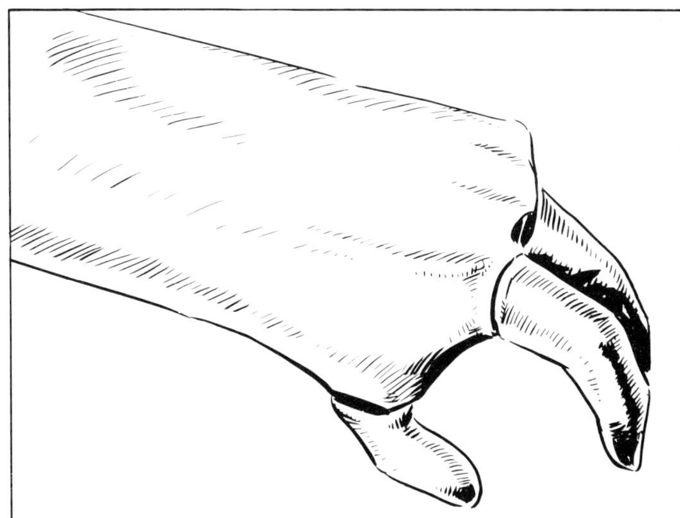

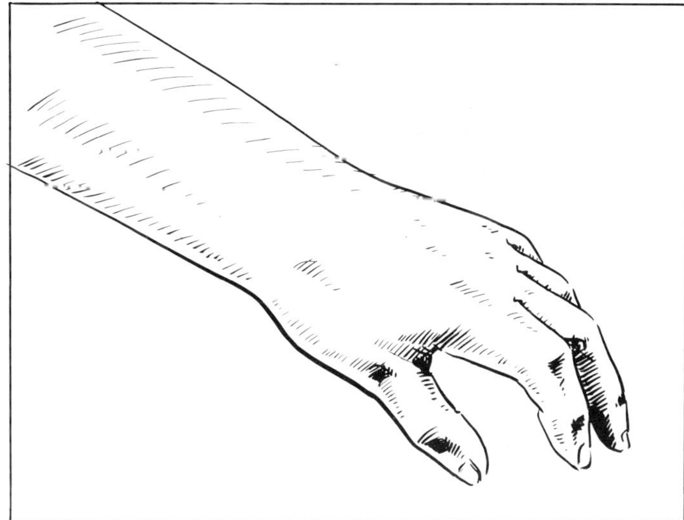

▲ This artificial arm and hand is made possible by advances in electronics. The mechanical piece seen above is attached to the nerve endings in the arm muscle. A tiny pulse (like an electric current) comes from the nerve endings and operates the moving parts. The controls are hidden inside a plastic arm and finally covered with a PVC glove to give it a natural look.

◀ This girl has a very advanced artificial arm which is linked to the nerve endings in her own arm.

One way to cut down the doctor's travelling time would be to use a home doctor computer. It might be possible to have a check-up while the doctor stays in his surgery and you stay at home or in the office. You will be able to see and hear each other through the videophone. The doctor will have your medical history on tape. Your computer terminal will be linked to his. It will be able to check your pulse, take your temperature, measure your heart beat and blood pressure and lots more.

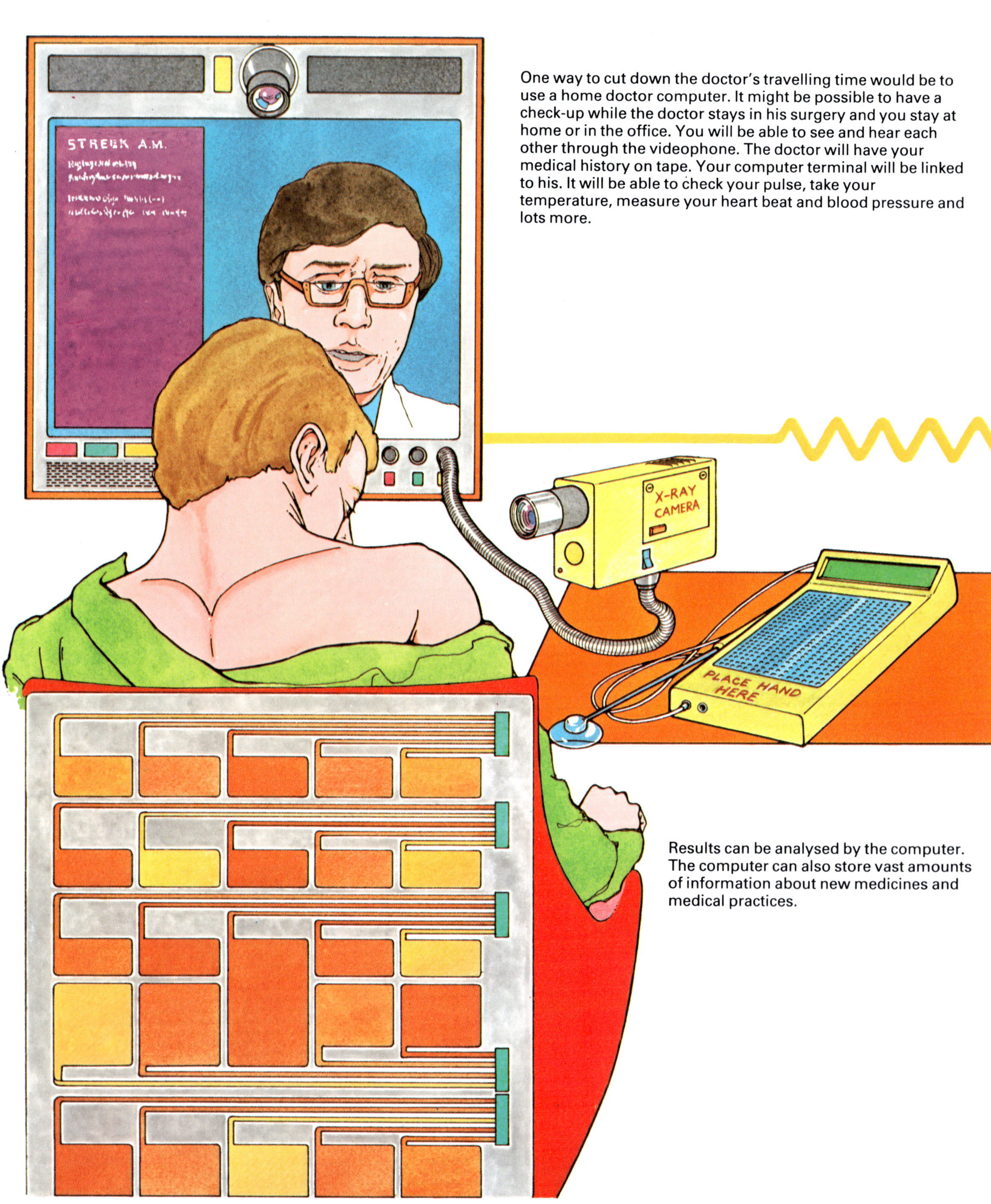

Results can be analysed by the computer. The computer can also store vast amounts of information about new medicines and medical practices.

Now, however, artificial limbs can be controlled with the aid of micro-chips, which help them move about normally. Although they are not like brand new arms or legs, they are certainly better than the hook which Captain Hook used instead of a hand in Peter Pan!

But, why is it that a young salamander can grow a new leg and we cannot? Scientists, with the help of computers, think it has something to do with the way cells grow and divide. Our bodies, and the bodies of all living creatures, are made up of cells. Cells are very tiny, so you can only see one if you use a very powerful electron microscope which makes them look larger.

Scientists can now grow some species of plants from a single cell. To do this they take a cell from the plant and let it multiply until it has become a cluster of cells. This cluster of cells is put into a tissue culture, a sort of jelly in which cells can grow. After a while a completely new plant appears. If scientists can do this with plants now, is it possible that in the future they will be able to take a cell from someone's body and grow a completely new part to replace a damaged or diseased part?

Computers and powerful microscopes are not only helping in experiments in cell growth. They are also being used in other areas of medicine, such as micro-surgery, by which a baby's arm can be sewn back on after an accident. In research as well, computers are helping us find out more about how our bodies work.

A body scanner makes it possible to diagnose illness with greater accuracy than ever before. The moving beams of x-rays scan the patient's body and are linked to a computer so that the information can be displayed on a screen to be read by a doctor.

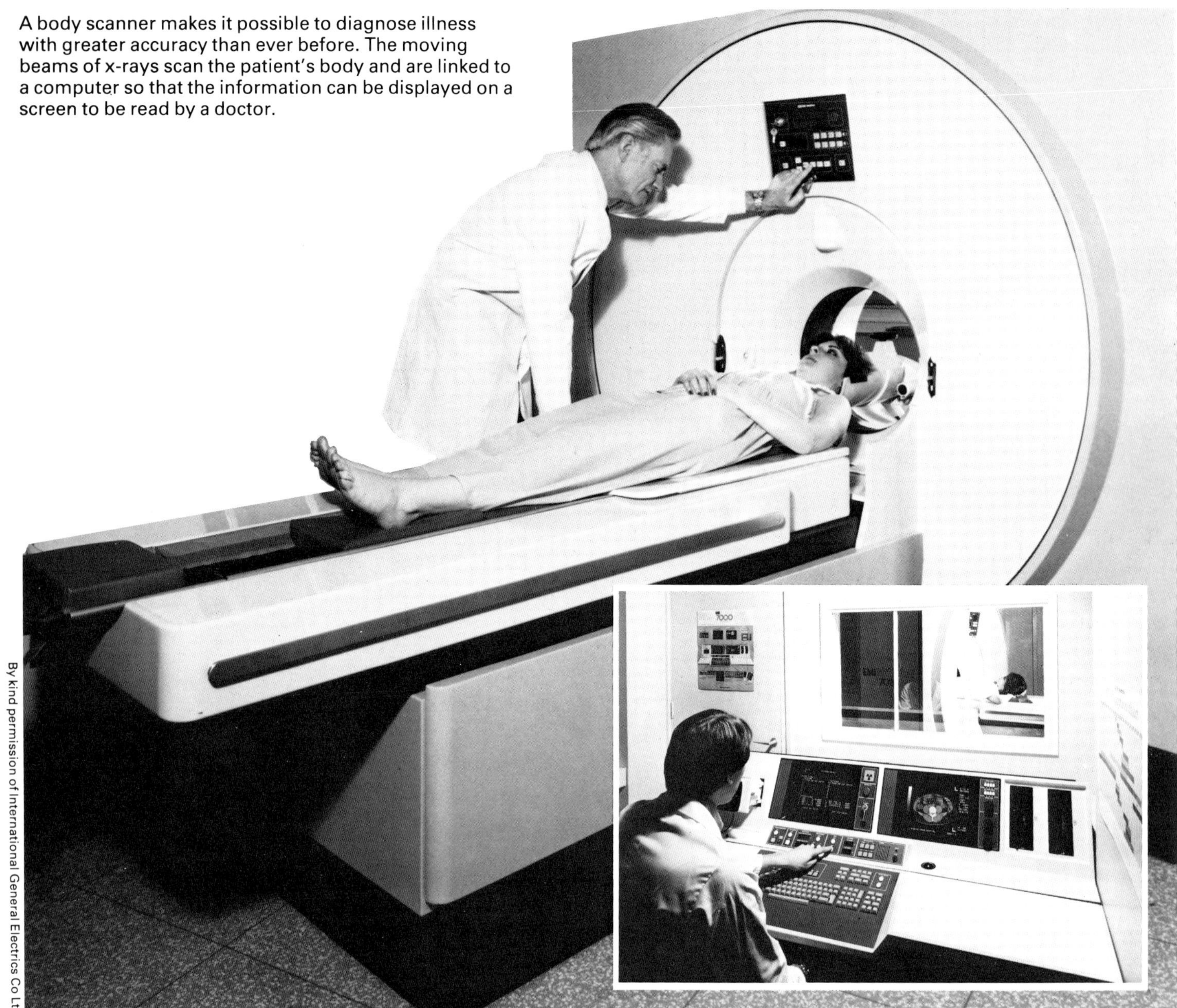

By kind permission of International General Electrics Co Ltd

All these new discoveries will mean that we should be living longer and healthier lives. Over the years we have been winning the war against disease and illness. A baby born today in Britain can expect to live until over 70 years of age. Babies born in 1900 were only expected to live to around 48 years of age.

Of course, we have to look after our bodies. They are rather like cars. If you don't drive a car too hard and if you keep the engine tuned and feed it the right petrol and oil, a car should run well and give little trouble. But a car has to be checked every now and then.

In the same way cars are checked, our bodies will be checked in the future. Micro-chips in special checking machines, or scanners, will let us know if there is anything wrong. Cars are taken into garages for a service about twice a year. In the world of the future you may be going along to a doctor for a service once or twice a year.

Stopping disease and illness is the best way of keeping our bodies fit and healthy. Micro-chips are helping to do this, but, of course, they will never take the place of doctors and nurses. A computer will not put on a bandage or pull out a splinter. But it can help us know more about ourselves. The more we know, the healthier we will be and the longer we should live.

In fact, because we are learning so much now, there is no reason why you should not live until you are 100 or 120 years old. So, be careful crossing the street – that could become the only way you will shorten your life!

A World Of Energy

Without energy we would not be able to live. There would be no plants, flowers, trees or grass. There would be no birds, animals, insects or fish. There would be no movement. All living creatures and plants need energy to grow, work and stay alive. Without energy there would be no life at all on Earth.

So energy is important. But, where does it come from, this energy we all need? The answer is not a simple one, because there are many different kinds of energy. When you lift a book from a shelf or write your name, you use energy. When you cycle you use energy. The longer you cycle, the more energy you use and you can actually feel it draining away as you become more tired. Finally you have to stop. If you rest and have something to eat, you will build your energy up again.

You can think of your energy as being a kind of store cupboard. When it is full, you can cycle quickly. As the cupboard becomes bare, you find cycling more difficult. But we can save our own energy by letting a car take us from place to place. But the car also needs energy. That energy comes from petrol. Petrol comes from oil, which we take from the ground or from under the sea.

Another kind of energy is electricity. When we turn on a light, energy is being used to light up the bulb. In a torch the energy is in the battery. As the energy is used up, the torch does not shine so brightly. When the battery has no more energy, we throw it away and buy another one.

But, suppose there were no batteries left in the shop when we went to buy one? Imagine there was no petrol left in the garages when your parents went to fill up the car? Suppose there was no light when you pressed the switch?

So how can we collect it? Scientists think the best way of collecting the fantastic amount of energy the Sun has to offer, would be to have huge panels in space, made out of thousands of photovoltaic cells. By the time you grow up, these panels should be in space, the energy from the Sun being beamed back to Earth, where it will be changed into electricity.

You will probably also have solar panels on the roofs of your houses. These panels will heat water as well as rooms. There will not be enough energy from these panels for all your energy requirements, but it will help you save the oil and gas you would have used.

Where else can we find energy apart from the Sun? Luckily there are lots of places here on Earth. Have you ever stood in the sea when the waves come racing towards you? The chances are that you have been knocked over. That shows you how strong the waves can be. Now scientists are looking at these waves to see if they can capture some of their energy.

Water has been used for thousands of years to provide energy. Water turned little pots on a large wheel to irrigate the fields of the ancient Greeks. The water from streams and rivers was used to turn millstones to grind corn and, of course, steam engines used water to make them work. Nowadays, some of the electricity we use is made by converting water, which is collected in areas of high rainfall, into electricity. This is called hydro-electric power, hydro meaning water, and it is one way of harnessing the energy from water.

Not only the Sun and the sea have energy. If we look hard enough around us, there are many different forms of natural energy. Some you cannot see, like the wind. But you can certainly feel it – it can knock down trees, as well as sail large yachts.

These houses in South London have been fitted with solar panels in their roofs. The panels provide hot water for the fourteen houses.

By kind permission of Energy Technology Support Unit

Windmills can give us electricity, but the problem is that we would need thousands of huge windmills as big as electricity pylons to give us as much electricity as we need. This would make some of our beautiful countryside look ugly. But, perhaps small windmills will become a common sight in the garden of the future, along with the solar panels in the roof of the house. A small windmill would not give enough power for all the house's needs, but it might recharge batteries, for example.

Batteries are very important because they provide a good method of storing electricity. Small batteries produce just enough electricity to run a torch, whereas large batteries can actually run a whole vehicle, such as a milk float. As we learn more about batteries, we can make them work better by improving the materials from which they are made. One method of keeping a battery working well is to recharge it from the ordinary house electricity supply or possibly from special windmills. This would be very useful, since by that time many of the cars you will drive will have batteries instead of petrol engines.

By kind permission of Energy Technology Support Unit

▲This large, electricity-producing windmill, properly called an aerogenerator, was built in Yorkshire at Aldbrough.

▼This hydro-electric power station in North Scotland (Pitlochry) produces electricity from turbines turned by rushing water. Here we can see the dam on the right and the power station on the left.

By kind permission of North of Scotland Hydro-Electric Board

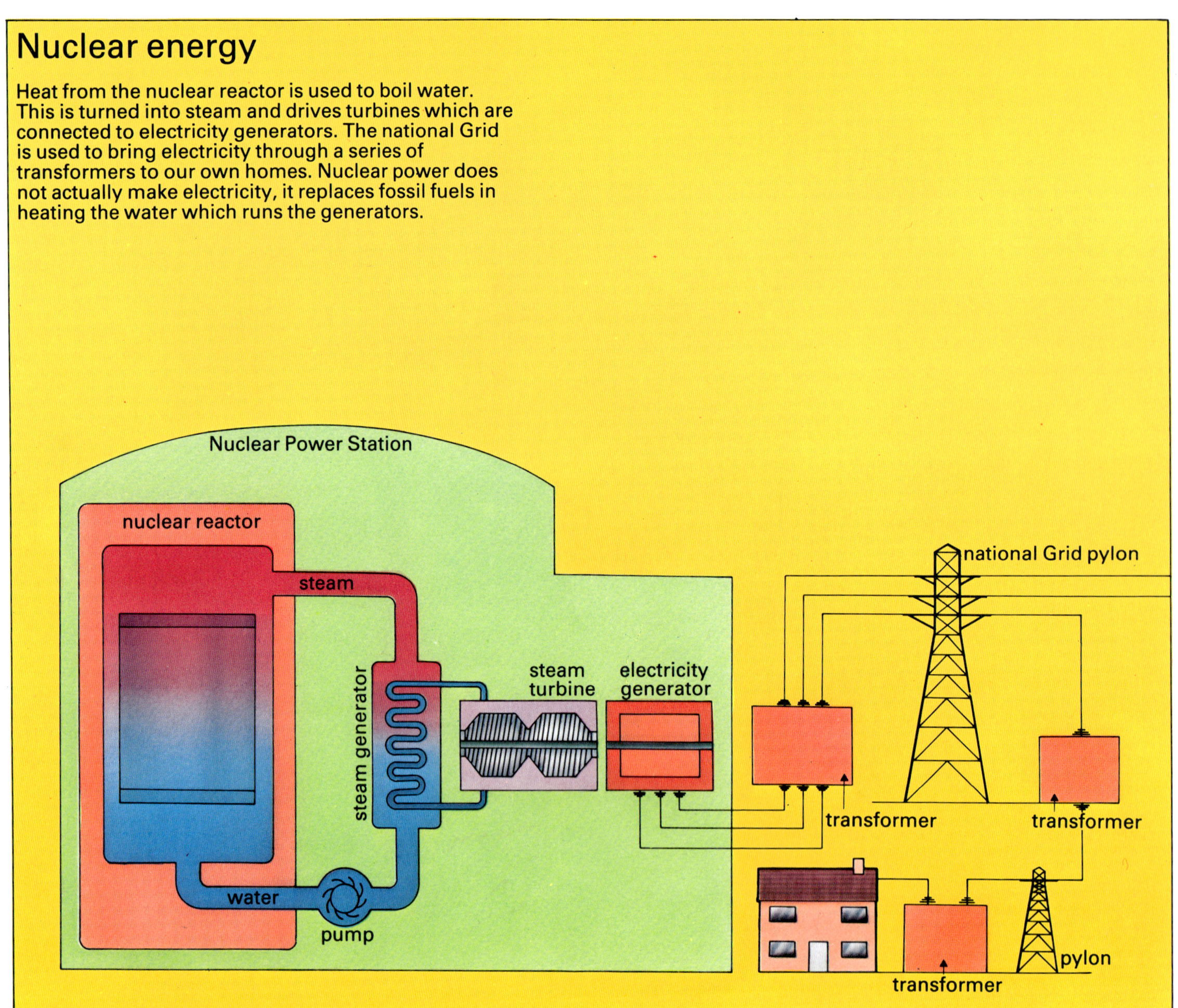

Another kind of energy has been found which needs huge machines to release it. This is nuclear energy, which at present comes from a metal called uranium. When the atoms of uranium are split up, fantastic amounts of energy are set free. In fact, two million times more energy than can be gained from the same weight of coal!

Everything in the world is made up of atoms. They have been called the 'building blocks' of the universe. We can only see them by using powerful microscopes. To give you an idea of how small they are, if 200 million atoms were put end to end they would measure just under 2½ centimetres! Atoms are held together by energy and we release this energy when we split an atom. It's called fission power. When scientists began to explore the world of atoms, many of the questions which had puzzled them for years were answered. For example, why are some things hot and some cold? The answer is that it depends on how fast the atoms are vibrating, or moving. The faster they move, the hotter something is.

Another puzzle was why doesn't the Sun burn up like coal or wood? What happens is that the Sun changes one kind of atom, called a hydrogen atom, into another kind of atom, a helium atom. As the change takes place, a fantastic amount of energy is released. This change is called fusion. We can change hydrogen into helium on Earth, but it is very difficult. When it happens quickly, there is an explosion. Controlling it is very difficult.

At the moment it costs too much to control and is no cheaper than any other kind of power or energy. If a cheap and safe way was found to 'fusion-burn' the hydrogen from the sea, we would have no fuel problems – ever!

But while nuclear energy can give us more than enough energy, many people are not happy about using it. For a start, it can be used to make bombs which could blow up the world. Also, once the uranium is used, it becomes radioactive, which means it can kill those who are near it. So it has to be buried or dumped at sea in special boxes. Some people say we cannot risk lots of people becoming sick or dying because of a uranium leak. Perhaps one of the jobs you will be doing when you grow up is trying to find a safe way of getting rid of radioactive uranium.

But, there are even more kinds of energy we can use. One of them is beneath our feet. It is called geothermal energy.

There are plans for a geothermal power station, which could be used to produce electricity. A large station, possibly moored at sea, could be used to pump water deep into the ground. The ground's natural heat will boil the water, which turns to steam. The steam could then be used in the normal way to generate electricity.

If you dug a very deep hole into the centre of the Earth you would find that it is extremely hot – on fire, even. This huge fire melts rock and sometimes this molten rock comes to the surface through volcanoes. We have already seen that by burning things, like coal and oil, we can use the energy trapped in them. In the same way all that heat in the centre of the Earth can be seen as another form of energy. If there was some way of gathering this energy, there is no doubt that it could become as important as oil. Already in some places around the world people are using steam from the centre of the Earth to give them electricity. In parts of New Zealand, factories, houses and hospitals are heated by geothermal energy.

At the moment we do not know all the places where we can tap this energy. But, because it is so important, a lot of work is being done to find them. If we can use all that heat and power beneath our feet, we will be able to solve many of our energy needs.

The Sun, the sea, the wind and the power in the centre of the Earth can give us an enormous amount of energy, if we can find ways of collecting it.

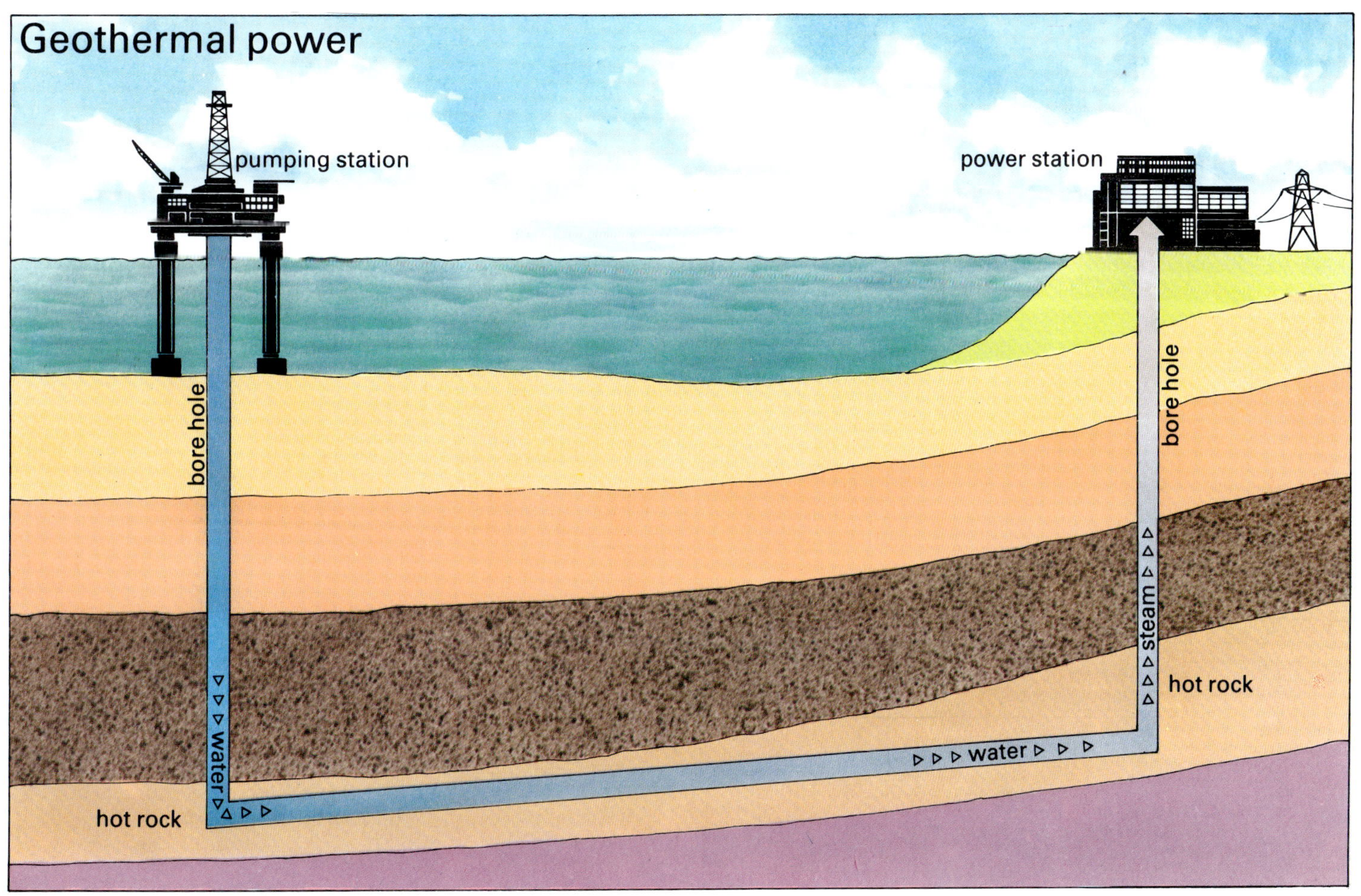

A tremendous amount of energy is wasted at the moment. We all waste energy without knowing we are doing it. Houses of the future will be built so that very little heat escapes from them. They will be insulated. On a cold day you put on a thick jumper or coat and your body stays warm – you are insulating your body. New ways are being found of insulating houses as well as saving energy in general.

We are very lucky that we have some help in trying to find answers to our energy problems – help that comes from micro-chips. Micro-chips use hardly any power, because they are so small and yet they can do fantastic amounts of work. Micro-chips are also being used to help us work out other ways of saving energy, by giving us extra thinking power.

Until now it has been easy to find the fuel and energy we need. We only had to dig into the ground for oil, coal and gas. Now it is becoming more difficult and dangerous and very expensive. Micro-chips can control robots in coal mines, as well as machines which pump oil out from under the seas and deserts. But we have seen that the energy cupboard is becoming bare. The days of cheap energy are over. But there is energy all around us and we have to find the best way of collecting it.

So far we have not mentioned an old form of power called steam power. A few hundred years ago an Englishman, Thomas Savery found that if you boiled water over a fire, the steam it produced could be used to drive pistons. This was how the steam engine was born.

The first steam engine used wood and later coal to boil the water. Steam from the boiling water was forced out through a kind of closed pot until it pushed a rod attached to a wheel. The wheels could then pull trains or make machines work. It was a marvellous way of saving our muscle energy.

Some countries in the world still use steam for powering engines, for example, the beautiful steam trains of India. But the most important use of steam in the world today is for producing electricity. We have seen that steam generators are an important part of a nuclear power station. Likewise they are an important part of most power stations.

No-one knows yet if other planets, like Mars, have fuel that we could use. We will soon know. Perhaps one day all the energy we need here on Earth will come from space, where, of course, all energy came from in the first place.

Rays from the Sun hit the huge solar panels of an orbital satellite, which contain photovoltaic cells. These produce electricity which is changed to microwaves beamed to a receiver on Earth. There the microwaves are changed back to electricity.

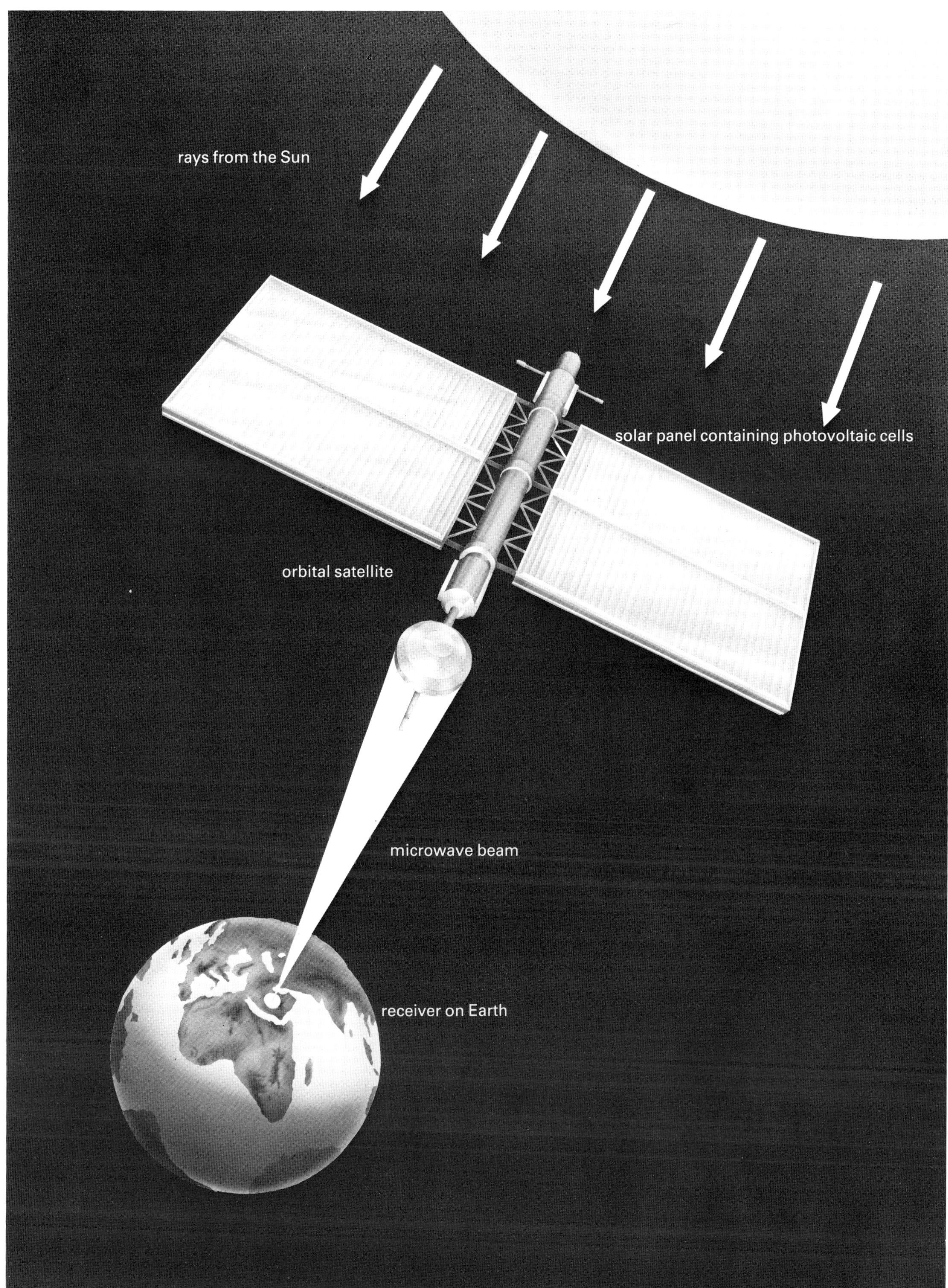
rays from the Sun
solar panel containing photovoltaic cells
orbital satellite
microwave beam
receiver on Earth

The Family Of The World

If you have friends who live on the other side of the world, it is not difficult to keep in touch with them. You can write and the letter should arrive a few days later. If you feel like talking to them, you can pick up a telephone. In a few years time you will be able to see your friends on special videophones as you speak to them. If you want to visit them, you can fly around the world. Actually, there is nowhere you cannot visit with permission. The pathways of the sky cover every country. The whole of the world is as close as your nearest airport.

It is difficult to imagine a time, about five hundred years ago, when most people thought it was impossible to reach the other side of the world. They believed the world was flat and if they went too far, they would fall off the edge!

Of course, we now know that this is not true. We know the world is round and we have even seen pictures of it from the Moon. These pictures were sent back to Earth with the help of micro-chips. The same kind of micro-chips are in the satellites which now circle the Earth and make it possible to speak to your friends on the other side of the world.

Satellites also allow us to watch on our television sets events that are actually happening at the same time as we are watching them. For example, we can watch a cycling race in France as it is being competed.

These satellites, which have made it possible to talk to someone on the opposite side of the world and to see live pictures from other countries, are in many ways bringing countries closer together. It is possible that when you are grown up your home computer could be linked not only to other computers in your own country, but also to computers all over the world, bringing the world even closer to you.

We can now travel about more easily and this is one of the reasons why it is also easier to build together. A hundred years ago, when steam engines were being built, all the materials and parts came from around one part of the country. For example, most of the trains used in Britain were built in Leeds, in the north of England. Leeds became the centre because nearly everything that was needed for the engines and carriages could be found near Leeds. Coal and iron came from mines around Leeds and were used to make steel. The wheels, engines and boilers were made from the steel in huge factories in Leeds. Cloth for the seats came from nearby.

If people in Britain ate and drank only what was grown and made in the country, their diets would be rather limited. They would be able to eat bread, because the wheat to make it is grown in Britain. There would not be enough bread for everyone, though, because we have to import (or buy into the country) large amounts of grain from countries like Canada which have more than enough for themselves.

There are certain foods that British people would not be able to get unless they were imported. Foods like bananas, oranges, rice and dates are brought into Britain from countries which can grow them easily. Rice, for instance, needs lots of rain and sunshine, so it is imported from countries like China. Drinks, such as tea and coffee are also imported.

It is not only food and drink that Britain buys. We also import things with which to make goods in our factories. Perhaps you are wearing a shirt made of cotton. It might have been made in a factory in Britain, but the cotton with which to make it was probably grown in India.

Rubber to make tyres, the soles of shoes, wellington boots and all sorts of other things has to be imported from another country.

Many of the packets, cans and kitchen equipment in this picture could have come from abroad. If you look around your kitchen at home you will find many products and equipment that have been imported. Most of them will have a label stating the name of the country in which they were made.

If you look at a map of the world, you will see how far and from which countries food and drink and other products have been brought to arrive in your home.

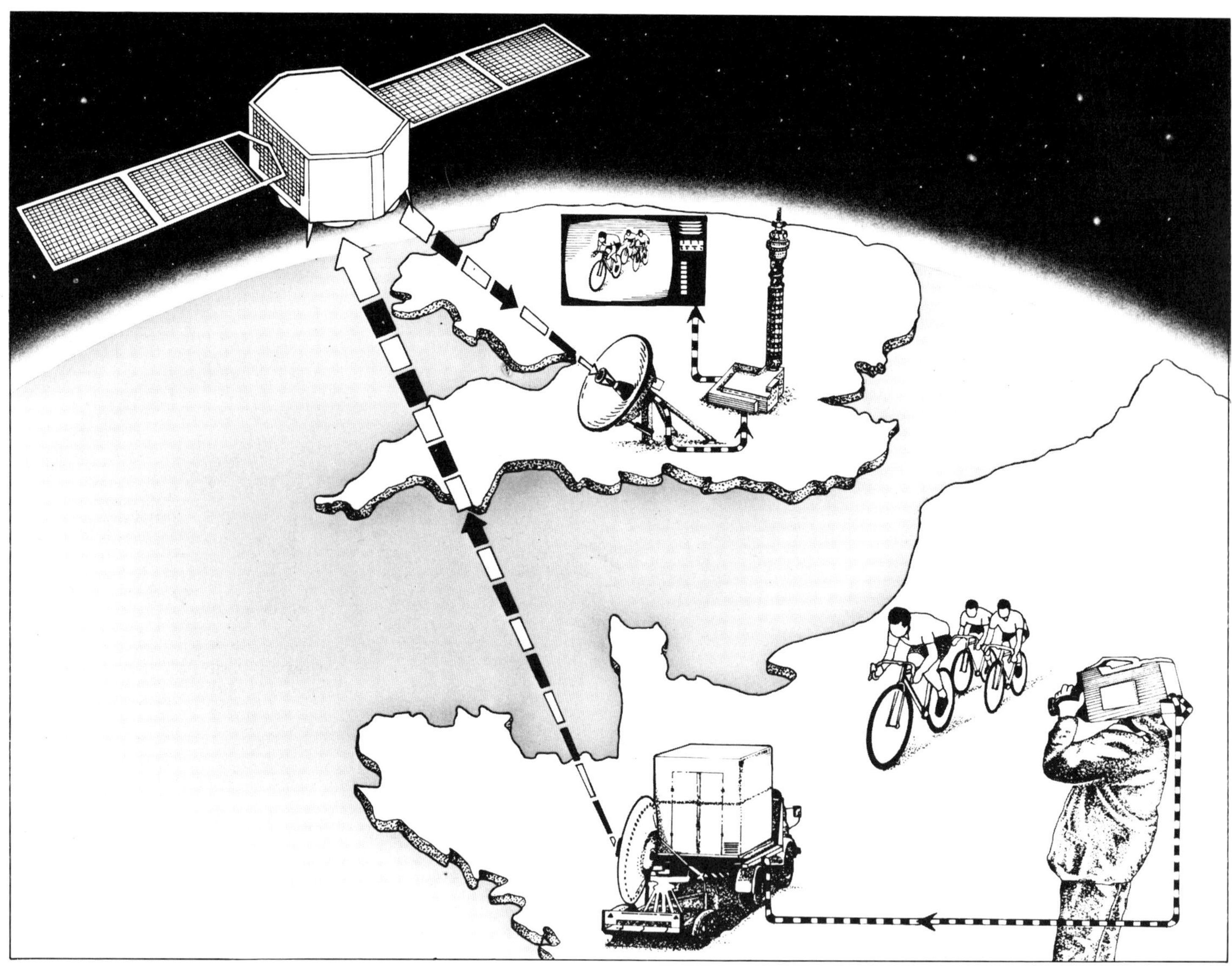

Live pictures are beamed from a transportable land station to the communications satellite. The satellite relays the signal to a receiving aerial in Britain. The picture is then switched by the Post Office Tower in London to your television screen.

Today, however, it is not nearly so important to have everything you need very close at hand. It can now be cheaper and easier to bring aluminium, a kind of metal used in building aeroplanes, around the world than it would be to use other metals found nearer the place the plane is to be built. The men who built steam engines had everything on their doorstep. For the men who build aeroplanes, the world is their doorstep.

Using materials from around the world leads to a greater knowledge of other countries and this can bring us all closer together. We are beginning to work, build and share together. Britain has joined a sort of club in Europe made up of France, Italy and, at the moment, six other countries. It is called the EEC (European Economic Community) or Common Market. All the member countries want and need the same things – energy, food and to build together.

As we have seen, micro-chips have helped and will help to make things better for us all, if we use them wisely. However, they have also been used in a way which could be very dangerous. They are being used in the making of weapons and bombs which armies, navies and air forces feel they need to make themselves and their countries stronger. Micro-chips have made it possible to send a bomb many thousands of miles to another country to blow up a city or army base.

This is the other side of micro-chips and it is not very pleasant. We now have enough bombs in the world to kill every single living creature – every man, woman, child, animal, fish and bird. In fact, it is now possible to blow the Earth to pieces, leaving nothing of it in space.

Have you ever wondered why countries go to war with each other? The usual reason for war is that one country has something another country wants – food, oil, gold and land, for example.

Hundreds of years ago, when countries that we know today were divided into smaller countries and regions, fighting broke out frequently as one region overran another to capture more land and food.

We have already seen how farmers with the help of machines can grow more food using fewer workers. Machines with micro-chips are making the things we need. So there is now no need to go to war with another country in order to have enough for ourselves.

But this can only work if all the countries in the world have enough and we know that this is not what is happening.

The richer countries of the world are much less likely to go to war than the poorer countries, because they have enough food and fuel or enough money to buy these necessary things. These richer countries, like Britain, Germany, Japan and the USA, are lucky.

But there are many countries where there is not enough food or fuel. In these countries children die every day because they do not have enough to eat or drink. At the moment about half the people in the world do not have enough food. Even worse, nearly all of the food in the world is eaten by only one quarter of all the people, who live in the richer countries.

These poor countries do not only need money, though, of course, this is important in times of famine. It would be far better to try and stop the famines altogether and this means having the ability to grow enough food to feed everyone.

We have to close this gap between the richer and poorer countries, if only to lessen the threat of war. Weapons are becoming more powerful and also cheaper, which means that poorer countries might soon be able to afford such terrible weapons.

How can we close this gap? Scientists, with the help of computers are trying to solve the problem. One experimental way that has already been found is to feed people a diet of mussels. Mussels are found clinging to rocks on beaches in many parts of the world and scientists have found that they are very rich in protein. Protein is something which is necessary for us to live healthily and which we in the richer countries get from eating food like eggs, cheese and meat. If people in the poorer countries could be taught how to farm mussels, it would go some way to solving their food shortage.

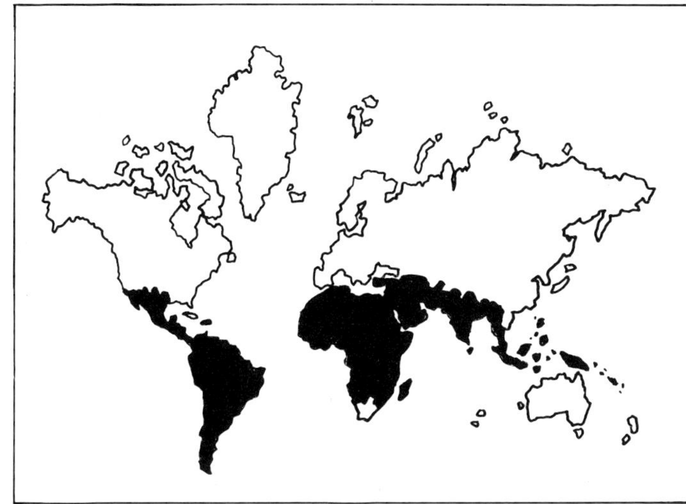

The black areas show the poorer countries, known as the Third World. These are the countries that need a lot of help from richer countries to conquer famine and disease.

If we can find answers to the problems in the poorer countries, as well as answers to our own troubles, like finding work for those who have none, then the future looks good. Instead of lots of little countries all facing their own problems, we can share and hopefully make these problems less. We are beginning to join together with other countries, which in many ways will help to make the world a smaller place.

There is a lot of work to be done before the world is free from trouble. Micro-chips are giving us extra thinking power, making it easier to help others. But having computers does not mean the world will be a better place. What it does mean is that there is now a chance to put an end to war, to killing and to hunger. It means that the 21st century has a chance to be one of peace. Whether you take that chance is what living in the future will be all about.

Transport

Over the last few hundred years travelling has changed a great deal.

About two hundred years ago roads, even main roads joining large towns, were very difficult to travel on. They were covered with pot-holes which in bad weather would fill up with water. The terrible state of these roads made travelling slow and very uncomfortable. In 1712 if you wanted to travel from London to Edinburgh the journey would take 13 days by stage-coach and cost £4 10s (£4.50). That was a lot of money in those days when 2½d (1p) could buy a loaf of bread. Roads began to be improved because getting from one part of the country to another became much more important, both for people and for goods.

About 150 years ago the steam train was invented and the system of railway lines began to be built up. This made travelling much quicker. In fact so much quicker that in 1870 the journey from London to Edinburgh could be accomplished in only 10½ hours and cost £1 12s 8d (£1.63).

Now, of course, we can travel by aeroplane in a faster time than ever before. London to Edinburgh by air takes only 1 hour and 10 minutes and costs £47. This sounds a lot more than £4 10s, until you think it is the equivalent of 117 loaves at today's prices. The stage-coach journey cost the equivalent of 450 loaves at 1712 prices.

Getting to your destination more quickly and more comfortably makes travelling much more pleasant, but there are disadvantages about aeroplanes as well. Pollution is one, and another is wastage of fuel. An aeroplane flying from London to Edinburgh uses 6,364 litres of kerosene, which is paraffin oil. As we saw earlier, saving fuel is very important if we are to make it last as long as possible.

This is one area in which micro-chips can help. They can be put into engines to keep them running smoothly, to let us know if anything is wrong and to control the amount of fuel going to the engine. So the micro-chip will help us to avoid wasting any fuel.

In what other ways will the micro-chip help us? Well, it is hoped that the micro-chip will keep buses and trains running on time. If we could be sure that buses and trains would arrive when they should, perhaps more people could be persuaded to travel by public transport rather than use their own cars. This would be another way of saving fuel. Computers are used to control flights at the moment, so it is not too far-fetched to expect computers to control buses

Which of the following fuels provide the energy for each mode of transport on the opposite page?

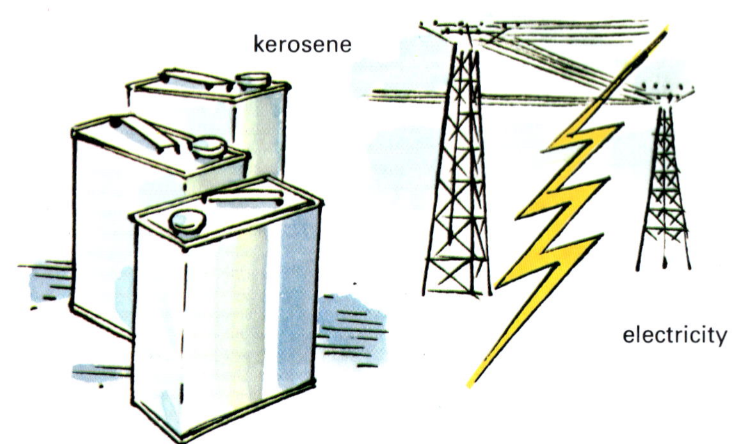

and trains here on the ground.

Micro-chips will probably also be used to improve the performance of cars. There are several ways in which this could be done. Already certain cars have been fitted with a computerised dashboard, which can give the driver all sorts of useful information about his car, such as when to change the tyres. Other improvements are likely to follow. Micro-chips could be used to control a car's electrical system. They might also automatically dim the headlights when another car is coming in the opposite direction. Another possible improvement is a device to make sure the wheels of a car do not lock, making sure it doesn't skid.

The micro-chip could improve travelling by making cars safer and more efficient and, perhaps, by controlling public transport to make trains and buses run on time. But it probably won't greatly alter the appearance of all these forms of transport.

There is, however, one area where we might see a totally new way of travelling – the mono-rail. There are already mono-rails working in Britain – one is running in Blackpool. A mono-rail carriage moves along a few centimetres above a single rail, propelled by a strong, magnetic **current** between the rail and the carriage. There is no noise or dirt and, of course, the ride is very smooth. The rail is about a metre off the ground on strong supports.

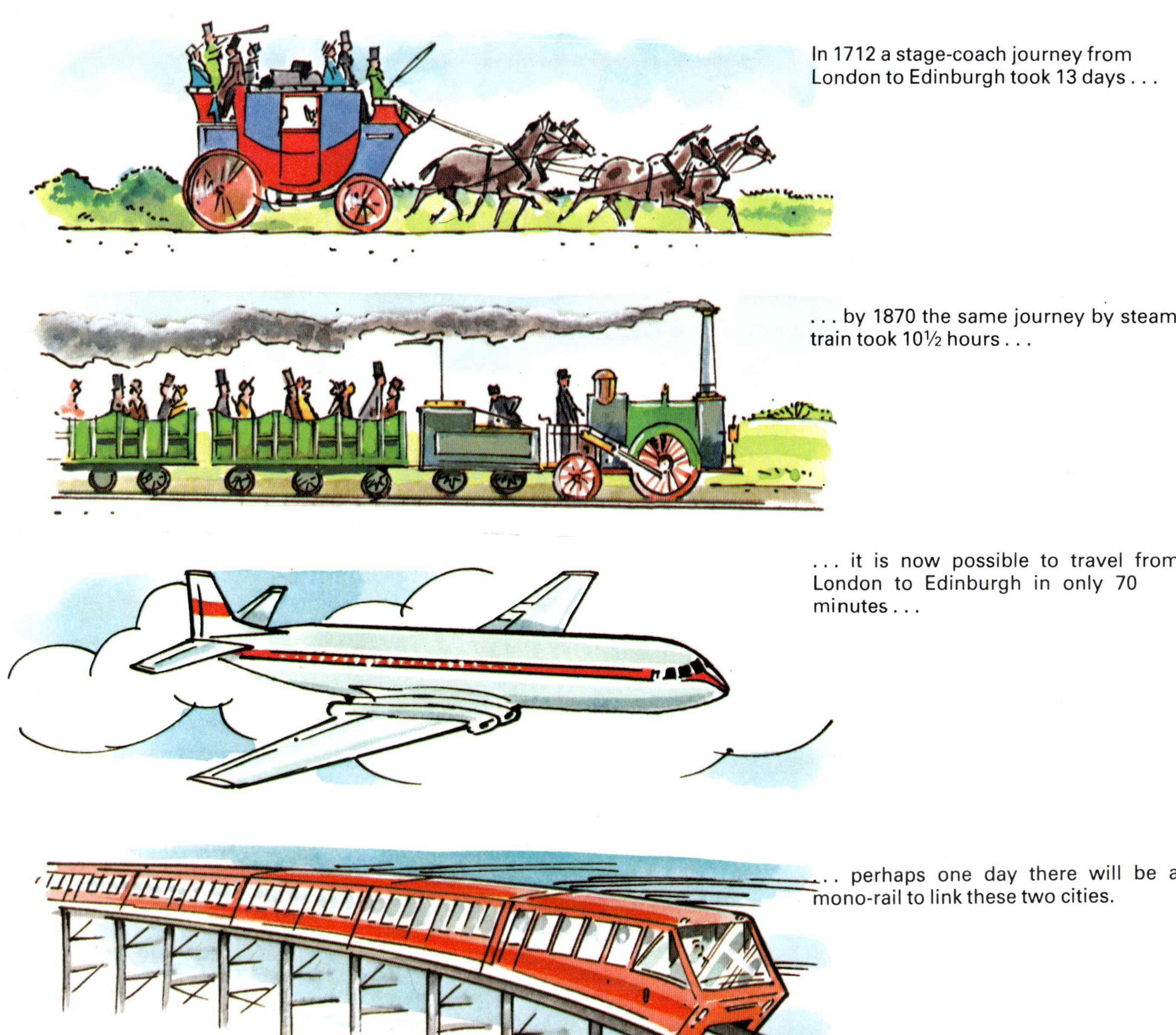

In 1712 a stage-coach journey from London to Edinburgh took 13 days . . .

. . . by 1870 the same journey by steam train took 10½ hours . . .

. . . it is now possible to travel from London to Edinburgh in only 70 minutes . . .

. . . perhaps one day there will be a mono-rail to link these two cities.

Glossary

Below are explanations of some of the more difficult words used in this book.

circuit A number of electrical parts joined together to make a complete path. A circuit carries electricity around it like a pipe carries water.

current The flow of electricity from one point to another is called an electric current. Such a current needs metal of some form to carry (or conduct) it along.

electronic An electronic machine is one that is powered by electricity.

mechanical A machine is a working arrangement of wheels, levers, cogs and other parts. The word mechanical describes something which is machine-like.

memories In the world of computer memories are devices by which information can be stored. In the case of micro-computers, a single memory chip contains all the stored information.

printed circuit The name given to a circuit of metal that has been designed ready for transistors to be slotted in. Here the word printed does not mean the same as ink on paper, it merely means the circuit was laid down in a prearranged manner.

transistor A transistor is a device which contains a crystal and fine wires. It increases the size (or amplifies) an electric current.

valves Valves are closed glass tubes containing electrodes. Electrodes are metal wires which carry (or conduct) an electric current.

word processor A word processing machine can store on a chip a vast amount of information relating to such things as spelling, spacing, punctuation and even translating. When used with a typewriter, the processor will correct most mistakes itself.